THE HOLY WAR AGAINST
HOMOSEXUALS

T. Stetson Hunter

BALBOA
PRESS
A DIVISION OF HAY HOUSE

ISBN: 978-1-4525-3225-7 (sc)
ISBN: 978-1-4525-3226-4 (e)

Balboa Press books may be ordered through booksellers or by contacting:

Balboa Press
A Division of Hay House
1663 Liberty Drive
Bloomington, IN 47403
www.balboapress.com
1-(877) 407-4847

Because of the dynamic nature of the Internet, any Web addresses or links contained in this book may have changed since publication and may no longer be valid. The views expressed in this work are solely those of the author and do not necessarily reflect the views of the publisher, and the publisher hereby disclaims any responsibility for them.

The author of this book does not dispense medical advice or prescribe the use of any technique as a form of treatment for physical, emotional, or medical problems without the advice of a physician, either directly or indirectly. The intent of the author is only to offer information of a general nature to help you in your quest for emotional and spiritual well-being. In the event you use any of the information in this book for yourself, which is your constitutional right, the author and the publisher assume no responsibility for your actions.

Any people depicted in stock imagery provided by Thinkstock are models, and such images are being used for illustrative purposes only.
Certain stock imagery © Thinkstock.

Printed in the United States of America

Balboa Press rev. date: 01/27/2011

He took that last step as half-man and half little boy, in his innocence of youth he didn't realize how that last step would affect so many others!

That last step must have been so hard for him to take when he knew he was leaving behind his parents who loved him so....

But this little half-man, half-boy was in so much internal pain, all he could think of was to stop the pain, dear God, how to stop the pain... of being classified an "enemy combatant" in this dreadful Holy War against Homosexuals.

Now what was once this sweet and very loving half-man, half-boy is the True Little Angel God created him to be! Finally at rest, this little Angel is in the protective arms of Jesus as Jesus now wipes all those little boy's tears away!

And Thank God that forever now with Jesus, Seth Walsh will never ever have to cry out in great pain like he did, when he took his last little step, no not ever again!

This book is dedicated to the memory of this sad and very confused little boy! Yes, a little boy who took such a giant step that he could never turn back from. And with that last very tragic step Seth Walsh showed the whole world he was... no longer willing to fight!

CONTENTS

A Holy War in Oklahoma

O nce upon a time there was a most wonderful God and this most powerful of gods created all things good. This loving God created very many things to be admired but the thing that this God loved the most was when, not wanting to be alone, He created His Own True Children. But one dark stormy night His Children fell fast asleep and during this sleep they, for the first time, dreamed. And while feeling all afraid and falsely abandoned in this lonely dark dream a devil did finally appear. This devil's name was Satan. So, while the God of love created many cherished things the only thing that Satan could create was a hell out of hate! Then out of that hate Satan did bring forth the false promises of many unending wars. These False Wars were destined to tear all of God's Good Children apart. Therefore in this sad satanic dark dream the devil was able to convince many of God's loving Children that their only purpose in life was to make of war a "holy" experience! So after many hate-filled eons and eons it is here our tragic story, in earnest, regretfully begins....

Yes, it's now official, there's been a longstanding and much debated Holy War declared in Oklahoma, U.S. of A. It was pronounced to be in effect as of March 1st 2006 by the Oklahoma Gazette. The newspaper's cover story and subsequent intelligence briefing were written by war correspondent Scott Cooper. His story begins: "Holy War. Conservatives are at their zenith of power following historic gains in the 2004 elections. But the new Republican majority in the House of Representatives has more in mind than just cutting taxes and reforming torts. Some legislators think they're on a mission from God." Yes, "A

1

marriage between politics and religion has been consummated. But the crusaders are not masking their intentions. They are riding through legislation with bravado and headlights. From the speaker of the House on down to his disciples, revivals are taking place in every meeting room of the Capital. "Is the House more religious conservative today than it was before? Speaker Todd Hiett asked rhetorically. "Absolutely yes."

"While the House leadership may have economic and judicial priorities, the legislative rank and file have moved moral values up the chart."

"Republicans with a Christian agenda are definitely the players in the Legislature, at least in the House," said Bob Darcy, a political science professor at Oklahoma State University. However, Darcy pauses before declaring the House a Christian state due to Republican control: "Oklahoma has been a pretty conservative state with this agenda for quite some time. It's not something Republicans invented. It might be new in the beating of the chest."

And as I'm now personally drafted into this drama by the announcement of a religiously based holy war in Oklahoma, I continue reading further on into this warning of a dire war story during which controversial Oklahoma State Representative Sally Kern is introduced.

Mr. Cooper writes, "Kern's first entrance on the stage of public notoriety didn't come in a legislative committee or on the House floor. It was at a public library a year ago when a parent found her child reading a gay-themed children's book. The parent called Kern, who began exerting pressure on the Oklahoma County Library Commission to remove the book from the children's section. Now Kern is attempting to take her gay-book crusade statewide. This session she introduced House Bill 2158, which would forbid the Oklahoma Department of Libraries from distributing funds to any public library that has not placed gay-themed books away from children's sections. It is similar to a resolution passed in the House last year.

But the former high school government teacher says she is a tolerant person.

"Somebody who wants to practice homosexuality, they have the right to do that," Kern told the Gazette. "They don't have the right to impose their beliefs on small children or anybody else." Her statement may seem simple enough, but on a New York radio talk show last summer, Kern made it quite clear what she thinks of gay people."I believe, like the Bible says, that we're all born with a sinful nature and capable of choosing the right path," Kern told talk radio host Michelangelo Signorile, "I don't believe people are born gay."

Then as I personally wonder if in Sally Kern's eyes "the right path" is only "her path," I am forced to continue reading on – especially since I DID NOT CHOOSE to be gay.....

"Back in the Legislature, Kern continues to toe a fine line between tolerance and crusading. She tells fellow lawmakers she doesn't want to teach intelligent design but does all she can to slice away at evolution. She proclaims people have the right to be gay, but calls homosexuality a sin.

Kern emboldens the Christian conservative wave in the state House and doesn't pretend to deny legislating morality. "Anytime a bill is made, somebody's morality is being legislated," Kern said. "That's just reality. While debating her bill on religious freedom in schools, Kern dissolved any questions about her stance on the separation of church and state. "It's an imaginary wall," she said."

So now I'm starting to see, after reading thus far in this informative story, who is partially responsible for fanning the flames of this declaration of Holy War when in Scott Cooper's article we are all finally introduced to - the Warring Class - a.k.a. the "Cultural Warriors" Mr. Cooper's article continues....

"When asked if her intent was to bring Christian values to state government, Rep Kern didn't hesitate. "I was running (for office) based on cultural, social issues," she told the Gazette. "I was running as a Christian candidate.

"I'm a cultural warrior. Is that my emphasis? Yes. But that's who I am."

"Kern is certainly not the first warrior to reside in the House. In fact, the man she replaced was known as one of the most unabashed Christian conservative lawmakers in state history – Bill Graves. How closely does Kern resemble Graves? She not only moved into his House seat, she moved into his former house in Windsor Hills. But Graves was a lone shepherd, left to his biblical tirades, which made great quotes but won few votes. Kern is one soldier among an infantry of holy warriors.

Practically all members of the 50th Legislature go to church and list it on their Web site bios. Several though are high-ranking churchgoers including deacons and pastors, mainly Republican.

Even more noteworthy is the bulk of ministers preaching legislation who were elected either in 2002 or 2004, creating the Christian conservative block. Among the more recently elected pastors are Rep. Dale DePue and Rep Paul Wesselhoft. They join Rep. Gus Blackwell who was voted in four years ago. Shawnee Baptist minister Steele is chairman of the House Health and Human Services Committee, which ushered in the abortion bills. Nance, chairman of the Public Safety and Homeland Security Committee, is also an ordained minister.

Reynolds brought his Baptist deacon credentials with him to the House in 2002, followed two years later by Rep. Phil Richardson. Rep. Ann Coody is married to an evangelistic singer while Kern's husband pastors the Olivet Baptist Church in Oklahoma City."

It's at this point in reading Scott Cooper's article that I realize more fully why he wrote early on in his war correspondence that, "A marriage between politics and religion has been consummated." I guess it's true, with Sally Kern acting as an official Oklahoma State Representative who is also married to and acting in the interests of Rev. Steve Kern who is preaching his gospel as a Baptist minister of God –along with Mr. and Mrs. Kern and the rest of the holy warriors - it finally tears me in two, as a gay man and as a Christian - when Scott Cooper's article on the Holy War in Oklahoma concludes with, "From the Bible to state statute." Yes, I can see why this news coverage is shaping up to be definitely, breaking news!

Mr. Cooper writes, "What may seem odd, and may explain the difference between a Republican and conservative Christian is the GOP traditionally stood for less government intrusion in personal lives. Kern said she and her colleagues have no choice: "When we get away from morality – when people don't have inner restraints, you have to rely upon outer restraints to control them. I'm not trying to impose Christianity down anybody's throat. What I am trying to do is bring back a sense of morality and of values that this country was founded on and we pretty much went by until the 1960's." Kern believes American society has become too open and accepting of beliefs that are out of the mainstream of traditional values, and that Christianity is the answer:

"Our country is the only country that allows freedom of religion. Why? Because in my opinion, and I think there is evidence to document it, it's based upon Christianity."

Then as I finish up with reading Scott Cooper's Holy War coverage, I slowly put the newspaper down and I have to ask myself as a gay male Evangelical Christian: Is Sally Kern right in that America allows freedom of religion because America is based on Christianity? But with me being fully aware of the fact that there are many different and diverse forms of Christianity, I can't help but to question what brand of Christianity is Sally Kern promoting? Is her style of Christianity based on her own personal choices of favorite passages she seeks for only to be found in the Holy Bible? But I guess for me to really get at the heart of all this dissention I have to ask if her version of Christianity is based on only the teachings of Jesus the Christ? So, I'm forced to ponder, what kind of Christian IS Sally Kern in Jesus' eyes? Right now, between the public Sally Kern and the private Sally Kern, I believe only Jesus knows what's in her heart for sure. Yes, only Jesus knows what's really behind the Cultural Warriors motivations to declare the need for such a un-Christ-like war.

And yet with the proud conservative beating of the war drums and a battle cry of "we're fighting for Christ" it seems not just Oklahoma but all of America is now tragically caught up in this major crisis by being vocally and financially engaged in an officially sanctioned ideological state of war. It's here this Holy War conflict is to escalate in earnest because with the Cultural Warriors very first shot condemning homosexuality – I realize, I'm not supposed to be judging them anymore than they are now supposed to be judging me! Oh, what a hell for us all!

With me being an Evangelical Christian, I know the traditional code for behavior is W.W.J.D? So with me trying to be a good Christian and asking myself What Would Jesus Do, I think Jesus would like me to ask the Cultural Warriors W.W.J.C? In Christian code that means Who Would Jesus Crucify?

But since I already know the Cultural Warriors want to crucify homosexuals, in an attempt to get at the gospel truth, I have to ask the Holy Spirit not only - Who Would Jesus Crucify? But I also ask who would Jesus refuse to forgive? Who does Jesus judge against? The Holy

Spirit within me tells me the answers to those questions are: "No one, not one, Jesus would never ever crucify anyone for any reason!" The Holy Spirit reminds me constantly that Jesus came to heal the world of the lost and sick. Jesus came to give sight to the blind.

But because I am writing these words during the time of a very pivotal official State of War please remember my rebuttals are extended in the spirit of love - but also remember that the Cultural Warriors have declared a no holds barred "Holy War against Homosexuals" and this hell of a battle seems to be getting pretty darn brutal. This Holy War is now splitting not just Oklahoma but the whole Christian world definitely into two very extremely different camps of thoughts and beliefs and actions!

While identifying myself as a homosexual, to some, I may be just considered to be useless trash and damaged goods but thinking beyond just my own gay Christian experience - it does seem to me that Satan's stirring up a lot of hate and division amongst us all and I can't help but to wonder where did humanity get so off track from just understanding basic love? God only knows.

But logic tells me that just like there are two kinds of love i.e. unconditional love and conditional love, there's also now to be found - two kinds of Christians i.e. the False Christians and the True! How do I know this? I understand the two kinds of love because I've received both kinds and I now understand there are distinctly two different camps of Christians because I read my Holy Bible.

And to emphasize that because we are at war - it's important for all of us to know who our real enemy is… for the Bible warns us dreadfully so…

2nd Corinthians 13-15

"For such men are false apostles, deceitful workmen, masquerading as apostles of Christ. And no wonder, for Satan himself masquerades as an angel of light. It is not surprising, then, if his servants masquerade as servants of righteousness. Their end will be what their actions deserve."

So now with me using my God-given logic, according to this Biblical passage, it sure sounds like Satan and some of his False Christian apostles have infiltrated the Christian churches from very early on and it also seems likely that they're playing us against one another by promoting un-Christ-like egocentric judgment-filled feelings. Therefore I have to admit that the reason I wonder if people like Sally Kern are False Christians is because True Christians are only supposed to express perfect love! And since Sally Kern and the other holy warriors are so wrapped up in publically demonstrating their homosexual-hate and, of course, hate is the epitome of the anti-Christ and, naturally, ANY hate-filled love is a very - imperfect love, so maybe it's time for me to give credit where credit is due.

I give credit to Jesus Christ for teaching me about love and grace. But most of all, I love Jesus because He has taught me about not judging others so that my own sins might be forgiven. So yes - even though we are now all caught up in an official war zone and America is engaged in a very destructive spiritual civil war and yes — while I have seen the difference between conditional and unconditional love and more to the point - even though I know the Bible has clues to who is False and who is a True Christian and even though half the Christians in the world think that, as a gay man, I'm a sinner bound for hell — I now, from the bottom of my heart, refuse to hate those who hate me for being a homosexual. Yes, I'm now finally at peace and I know God loves me. Now I truly know God loves everybody. And, dear God, thank you so much for all of the professional mental therapy I've been so graciously given!

In addition, I love God because the Father in Heaven sent Jesus, to us, to teach us all that when the world decides to crucify you for whatever reason, crucify whoever is fashionable and in whatever season — it's crucially important to still follow Jesus' example and to offer love and give grace in return! So, with me writing this book and trying to now extend God's grace to those who hate me... I must always remember that when the world chooses to crucify me just because they want to condemn me and limit my image to just being "one of those fags" — I must remember the words of Jesus Christ on the cross......
""Father, forgive them for they know not what they do."

Yes Dear Father, they know not what they do to us as homosexuals; but ironically, they also don't realize what they do to their very own souls — when religiously conservative Christians act out of a deep inner fear by verbally crucifying and vilifying any of God's Children who are simply just creatively made different.

And now with the laser beam of focused awareness that Satan is trying to mastermind a Holy War that's hell for everyone, please strap on your survival gear while we all head out into the darkened wilderness of misinformation, misrepresentations, Satanic illusions, and battling human egos so that we can all join together, united in solidarity, as we all personally fight ONLY OUR OWN ever-seductive False Christian inner-demons!

So who is killing an innocent soul?

And, please pardon me, while I do constant battle with my own need to balance greater outward forgiveness while also still trying to inwardly separate the false from the true! Yes, with promoting hate or promoting love, sadly it seems, this earthly war of many different Christian concepts is now set up to continue, as the Daily Oklahoman on Sunday March 12th, 2006 in the newspaper's Your Views section printed an op-ed piece written by Regina D. Nelson. The title was "Molesters deserve to die." It's a very thought provoking title and according to Regina, "After reading the state Senate had passed a bill allowing the death penalty for repeat child molesters, I was elated. Sen. Jay Paul Gumm said it best: "We allow the death penalty for someone who kills the body. Why in the world would we let someone escape who has killed the soul?" Someone who preys on children doesn't deserve to live in our society. Perhaps if the death penalty were on the table the offenders would think twice before touching a child..... What's more important than protecting children?"

Then Regina profoundly asks, "What's the cost for mental health treatment and suicide for the victims?"

And as I read Regina's thoughtful, insightful question I think of the money invested in mental health treatments that have been spent on me to keep me from committing suicide. Writing from personal experience, I know in the past I've tried to commit suicide because of being abused and bullied. And for a shot of honesty, I'll admit that much of my past inner-pain has come by way of a society that has been programmed and taught by some religious leaders that because of their personal interpretations of Scripture I, as a homosexual, am to be considered an enemy of the state worthy of all of the laws that can be rationalized, in their minds, to strip away my freedoms and liberties. Yes, the glaring facts are: There are people right now in the world, even today, who feel that homosexuals deserve the worst kinds of punishments, many people around the globe even speak-out with the wish and desire that homosexuals could and should lose not just jobs and homes but also lose their very lives! Adding in the fact that people like this also claim to be acting as God's agents, hell-bent on destroying all homosexuals, has caused me such great pain that my only remedy was found in immersing myself with years of seriously intense mental therapy. But the craziest fact for me to have to fight with is the knowledge that, as my therapist has explained to me, there is absolutely - nothing wrong - with being gay or in my need to accept my own sexual orientation.

So yes in my mind, abuse is an ugly animal that Satan seductively unleashes on us all by way of those people who are sleeping within to the power of true Christian love and that, thank God, His Grace is always there for those who fully comprehend its sacred meaning.

But while we're dealing with the subject of abuse and the importance of protecting children, I have to admit that during the active process of my mental therapy I remember one day asking my therapist – which is worse – physical abuse or mental abuse? Is sexual abuse the worst? Or, are mind games the worst? Mind games like when people quote, "love the sinner but hate the sin" while you can plainly tell - they feel so superior to you - while they love to hate you for being gay. My therapist's response to which is worse, physical/sexual abuse or mental abuse: "They are the same, they are all abuse and are ALL equally destructive!"

It was with that answer I confessed to my therapist that the reason I was asking the question of "what is worse" was because there was a lot of media attention being vocalized about the Catholic Church and the way they were handling (or mishandling?) their clergy sex abuse problems. Ironically in the car on the way to my therapy session I was listening to the radio and there was a lot of controversy and anger spilling out over the radio talk show on the subject of the Catholic Churches' moral authority. That religious controversy got me to thinking of who in this war torn world of ours has final ultimate moral authority? Is it the church or the state or the A.P.A.? And as my mind started to go to wondering, it now has me starting to question – not just moral - but medical and legal authority, my God, who on Earth has the topmost authority? Who should we all listen to for true guidance especially when people's words and deeds don't match up? And as I continued on with all of my deep internal debates I had the thought that if in this world there is known sexual abuse and mental abuse then, God forbid, what about all the damage that's now done to innocent people by religious abuse? That's what I decided I needed to talk to my therapist about because sexually abused children aren't the only ones who commit suicide. And as I think of the people who claim to represent God and in their zeal and zest to convert other people to their own ways of thought what happens when in reality they kill someone's soul while coyly claiming they are only out trying to "save a soul?"

So now I can't help but worry about all of the young people, their families, and the communities around the world who don't have access to the education and counseling they all need to help them understand what being a homosexual is really all about minus the myths, misrepresentations, and demonizing. And yes, in our crazy world there is a lot of demonizing so I do wonder about all of the kids who, like me, have been negatively influenced by church leaders and preachers who ultimately teach gay children to hate themselves. Why does society, in general, allow some religious leaders and their organizations to mentally abuse homosexual children by letting those leaders, preachers, and their followers tell "those kinds of children" that homosexuals are inherently evil and perverted? What about all of the children who even today kill themselves because as they reach puberty they can't reconcile their sexuality with those traditional familial religious teachings? I do know that Jesus feels that all of our anger and confrontations over these issues are misapplied, misappropriated, and are totally counter-productive to nurturing a genuine grace filled love. And as I keep reading in the newspapers about some of the current high profile suicides performed by tormented gay kids, it just breaks my heart – especially as being someone who can so deeply relate to Jesus' unconditional love.

And forgive me for asking this but, now that we know from a professional therapist's point of view - sexual and mental abuses are the same - do the Cultural Warriors ever wonder if in Jesus' eyes they are equally destructive to Him as well? Yes, destructive not just to an innocent child but also very much destructive to Jesus Christ's core message of pure grace! As I think to myself: What if God really does understand, forgive, and unconditionally love even homosexuals? If God can and does love gays will all the people who have ever taught that "God hates Fags" will they one day be found guilty of murder by way of causing mental religious anguish to the point of suicide for so many children who one day realize they were just naturally born gay and that they are now "naturally hated"? Plus, what of those people who, to this day, abuse and even kill gays - all around the world - all on personal religious justifications? Are people like this to be given an award or punished? Or, should all of God's devote religious zealots just be given a free pass while being politely ignored? But I'm "naturally" becoming painfully aware that with all of these serious life and death abuse of morality questions now churning around in my head, this unholy war over people trying to be "holy" is starting to get so much more intense for us all.

But still I wonder, when and if the time comes and science can prove that homosexuals are genetically predisposed and are made this way like I, a gay person, believe – then, dear God, at that medical time of scientific proof will all the religious leaders and organizations that have ever spoken out about the evils of homosexuality be finally considered guilty of inciting unjust hate? By God will these people be found guilty of slander, because the Bible does talk in detail of the extreme sin of slander; but also, will humanity one day judge uncompromising hate to be worthy of the death penalty to be dispersed by the equal standards of all of the world's courts? And then as I think of how in this world we sometimes have to euthanize mad or vicious animals.... then sadly, while I admit can't speak for God or the courts, I do know in many people's minds right now so many religious leaders are all ready known to incite vicious hate to one level or another aimed at one group or another. So, in this world torn by Satan's many wars, we now just have to wait to see how the Supreme Court will eventually decide on the issue of the constitutionality of exercising and exhibiting unrepentant, unremorseful, soul damaging hate.

And yet, in matters of the courts, what about all of those teachers who claim to represent God - will traditional fundamentalist preachers who willingly promote false beliefs and preach unrelenting hate and discrimination against homosexual children and adults should they be tried and convicted, while being considered legally eligible for the death penalty, for mentally abusing so many innocent souls? Especially when the case is of someone - willfully and deliberately – promoting, by physical attack or pure unadulterated mental anguish, any homosexual's suicide? Of course with all these thoughts firmly in mind I reason that's why people who hate homosexuals so much don't want hate crimes laws to ever include sexual orientation. Then from the heavy side of my mind I wonder, if die-hard homophobes can't out right kill gays, like they did to Matthew Shepard, are people so afraid of homosexuals only satisfied if they can at least have the legal freedom to drive us to the point we kill ourselves…. like they did to 13 year old Seth Walsh, or Billy Lucas a 15 y.o. who hung himself on Sept 9th from the rafters of a barn, or Tyler Clementi an 18 y.o. who jumped off the George Washington bridge, or Asher Brown another 13 y.o. who shot himself in the head on Sept. 23rd or, dear God, the countless numbers who have gone before them or who are now destined to follow in those very tragic footsteps as way too young victims caught up in these very many sad UN-Christ-like Wars? So I'm forced to question what Jesus - really thinks - of those people who practice any form of persecution in Jesus' holy name?

But even with all of my own personal inquiries, adding in all of this internal and external fighting back and forth, as I try to delve into meaningful self-introspection I think on a higher level: Will even the courts of the world along with all of us – Yes, we the people - judge AND juror, will we all one day, at the time of "final judgment," be ultimately held accountable for all of the mental and physical pain anyone has ever suffered at the hands of those people who profess to love the Lord but then they repudiate and condemn any and sometimes all of God's many different children? If our sin is not one of commission is it one of blatant omission – of not boldly standing up for the common rights of all basic humans? Then I'm forced to think of all of this un-Christ-like controversial fighting over "saving souls" as being just so insanely crazy!

But I do wonder what the world will do when the time comes and we all finally do open our eyes and see the truth that there is innocent blood on many of the hands of some of our many diverse religions and their leaders, teachers, and promoters? And yet, while I'm still confused about a lot of things, that's one thing I can clearly see that all religions seem to have in common – they can abuse and they can be very abused, it's all in who's at the helm! And it seems that the reasons so many people are fighting all kinds of Holy Wars right now are because by righteous political decrees and the actions taught to us in the pews - for us to take in the voting booths - many piously religious people are still promoting the damage, in one way or another, to so many innocent children's souls!

So yes dear Father, please forgive us all - for all the many times we truly know not whose soul we crush and maim while You, The Most Holy One, are now forced to watch all of these very many different and very diverse Holy Wars without end share in the fact that these ungodly wars are destructive the most to little tiny children when they innocently sit in any house of worship and learn how to hate – OR ELSE… their punishment will be to be eternally hated!

And as I think of all of Satan's hate and how powerful and contagious hate can sometimes be I'm reminded of the words in John 16:1-3 Jesus said "All this I have told you so that you will not go astray. They will put you out of the synagogue, (and Christian churches) in fact, a time is coming when anyone - who kills you - will THINK he is offering a service to God. They will do such things because they have not known the Father or me."

So as I - think - back on Sally Kern's pronouncement about homosexuals, "They don't have the right to impose their beliefs on small children or anybody else," I wonder… if turnabout is fair play then: Is it true that pious homophobic Christians "don't have the right to impose their beliefs on small children or anybody else" either?

Therefore, with all of these very clashing thoughts, it seems this fight for what is morally right is now fully on… and that's for, all of us, "damned" sure!

CHALLENGING TIMES

Yes, it's very challenging being gay while living in a religiously homophobic world. It's challenging physically and mentally but to me it's especially challenging to be gay emotionally. I guess that's why I eventually had a mental breakdown and ended up seeing a therapist once a week for a little over three years. My therapy sessions struck a lot of highly sensitive and frayed nerves within me so it's very challenging for me to now write this book and to try and share my experiences and feelings with the world. But thanks to my therapy sessions I'm now doing a lot better emotionally and that's part of why I am writing this – maybe this book will help someone else to understand what it's like to be Christian and gay; but even more so, maybe this book will also help people who may be Christian and homophobic realize what cause and effect relationships are being so tragically intertwined.

Now, as the Holy Spirit convinces me that any hate IS just plain Satan's hate no matter who you justify directing it at, I find myself confused.

Yes, I have to admit that even after all of the years I've spent taking therapy sessions, I'm still confused. Yes, I'm very confused about how any minority can still choose to beat-up on any other minority. It really confuses me anytime I see African-Americans and Hispanics being homophobic. With me being a gay white male born in the late fifties I've seen prejudice from both sides of the spectrum. Over the course of my life time, here in America, I've seen the prejudices some white people have expressed toward those they considered to be less than - the unequal ones, and for light-skinned people to be hateful or prejudicial

15

it's not something for any of us to be proud of. History has taught me about the great things humanity is capable of, but history also has a dark side to it - its Satan's side to it. And, of course, Satan doesn't care who we hate as long as we continue to hate; so, seeing how so many different minorities are treated, even in the 21st century, I guess it only makes sense that homosexuals are to be singled out for discrimination as well.

But, thank God, because of my being gay I've experienced what it's like to have prejudiced feelings turned toward me and by my seeing the ugliness of it I have vowed to eliminate all feelings of prejudice from within me. Prejudice now stops with me, no prejudice for any reason – against ANYONE! But still, I can't help but to wonder how anyone who has ever been shown prejudice can then turn around and willfully express prejudice toward others but I guess that's where my therapy has been so helpful. My therapist explained to me that when people are abused emotionally or physically they can get very frustrated and when they don't know how to mentally process that frustration the easiest thing to do is to turn around and pass that abuse and frustration on to someone else. My therapist told me that is why children who have been abused can many times grow-up to abuse. It's a learned behavior in response to all the abuse.

But I must admit that what confuses me the most is how people who claim to be Christian can be so prejudicial. I've seen all kinds of prejudices coming from Christians who have been lucky enough to be born into good families who love and take care of their children. Some of these people have never been mentally abused or physically hurt or felt prejudice used against them and yet they without ever experiencing real abuse themselves – they turn around and abuse those whom they think of as different. And I wonder if their repulsion and sometimes extreme hate comes from being seduced by Satan into thinking that they are superior just because of all of the good things that they have been lucky enough to have been given?

Yet, while I can't say for sure whether or not Christians who feel superior have all been seduced by Satan, I do know my therapy has helped me to understand a lot about how the world works. And as grateful as I am for my therapy, the Bible has helped me the most in understanding how God works! The Holy Bible has shown me how much God loves and the Bible has shown me how much God expects from us when we say, "I know God!"

1 John 2:3-6 "We know that we have come to know him if we obey his commands. The man who says, 'I know him' but does not do what he commands is a liar and the truth is not in him. But if anyone obeys his word, God's love is truly made complete in him. This is how we know we are in him. Whoever claims to live in him must walk as Jesus did." (But most importantly, we must love as greatly as Jesus!)

John 13:34-35 Jesus said, "A new command I give you: Love one another. As I have loved you, so you must love one another. By this all men will know that you are my disciples, if you love one another."

1 John 4:7-8 "Dear friends, let us love one another, for love comes from God. Everyone who loves has been born of God and knows God. Whoever does not love does not know God, because God is love."

1 John 19-21 "We love because he first loved us. If anyone says, 'I love God' yet hates his brother, he is a liar. For anyone who does not love his brother, whom he has seen, cannot love God, whom he has not seen. And he has given us this command: Whoever loves God must also love his brother."

But sadly in our minority hating and homophobic world it seems that Satan is still so able to limit the way we give love by limiting who we choose to see and call "brother!" 1 Peter 5:8 "Be self-controlled and alert. Your enemy the devil prowls around like a roaring lion looking for someone to devour."

And while the world still devours ethnic and religious minorities while proudly promoting the crucifying of homosexuals I read in Luke 6:32-36 "If you love those who love you, what credit is that to you? Even sinners love those who love them. And if you do good to those who are good to you what credit is that to you? Even sinners do that. And if you lend to those from whom you expect repayment, what credit is that to you? Even sinners lend to sinners expecting to be repaid in full. But love you enemies, do good to them and lend to them without expecting to get anything back. Then your reward will be great, and you will be sons of the most High because he is kind to the ungrateful and wicked. Be merciful, just as you Father is merciful"

So then I think of the sharing of mercy the same way I do about sharing love – does Satan now tempt us and stop us from showing mercy toward ALL people by limiting our view of mercy to only those people we feel are "good-enough" to deserve mercy? Does Satan teach us that mercy is only due to those people who look and act and worship like we do? Yes, I think that's one of Satan's main goals!

Yet it is written in Titus 1:15-16 "To the pure, all things are pure, but to those who are corrupted and do not believe, nothing is pure. In fact both their minds and consciences are corrupted. They claim to know God, but by their actions they deny him."

And thus, by their actions done out of extreme prejudice and hate do False Christians deny the reality that God is love…. When, in truth, the Bible clearly states "God is love!"

Therefore after I read all of these Biblical verses I wonder if the way Jesus saves us is not just by extending grace to us but also by teaching us so much about our own fallible human selves. Should the Holy Bible be considered to be human psychology 101? I ask this because "to the pure, all things are pure, but to those who are corrupted…. nothing is pure" and this again is where my therapy has helped me out so very much. I remember the day I asked my therapist, "How can people, who claim to be Christian, be so mean-spirited and call other people such horrible names while doing such horrible things to them?" It was then I learned about the power of PROJECTING and this is the very wise wisdom my therapist gave to me….

"Projection is the opposite defense mechanism to identification. We project our own unpleasant feelings onto someone else and blame them for having thoughts that we really have."

"A defense mechanism in which the individual attributes to other people impulses and traits that he himself has but cannot accept. It is especially likely to occur when the person - lacks insight - into his own impulses and traits."

"Attributing one's own undesirable traits to other people or agencies."

"The individual perceives in others the motive he denies having himself. Thus the cheat is sure that everyone else is dishonest."

"An individual who possesses malicious characteristics, but who is unwilling to perceive himself as an antagonist, convinces himself that his opponent feels and would act the same way."

So then I think of all of the people who presently think that the "homosexual agenda" is totally destroying our morals and nation. Yet, due to my current understanding of projection - I wonder if it's really the False Christians of the world who are destroying our morals and perverting the gospel of good news with its true forgiveness and love and expedient mercy? But it is then I realize I still need to forgive and love even all False Christians, whomever they may be, wherever they may be – damn it, we have all sinned… so now I have to repent of wanting to return hate for hate; and instead, I ask God in heaven to show the people who are still sleeping… there IS the potential Love of God at the heart of every individual. And dear God, please gently help those people "awaken" who are now unwittingly, sinfully seduced and caught up under the 'special' spell of Satan – and because we have all sinned please dear God give us all great mercy!

And yes, it seems that we may ALL have very challenging times up on ahead in our continuing effort to defeat that proud and prowling inner-beast called… I'm just "naturally superior" on a count of being such a special – "perfect Christian."

Then as I take an honest look all around me I wonder if with all of the hate Satan is raining down upon us all, are we all in danger of getting in way over our heads while so many people are now drowning in so much "moral" disgust? As I question, how many people are already getting carried away… by the flood of Satan's "SUPERIOR" hate? God only knows, but I have comfort – HE DOES KNOW!

But, for me, the most challenging thing I would now like to address is: After reading that Tony Perkins said that gay teens resort to 'depression or suicide' because they know they're 'abnormal'; well, if Tony Perkins who is President of the Family Research Council truly believes he has Jesus standing by his side would Mr. Perkins be brave enough to one day walk up to the President of the American Psychological Association and ask the President of the A.P.A. Dr. Carol D. Goodheart – from one "equal" President to another - what do the words, "When bullies blame their victims" truly mean?

Then as I seriously contemplate on who do I TRUST the most for the gospel truth about mental health – the President of the Family Research Council – or – the President of the American Psychological Association; the Holy Spirit within me tells me to NOT trust any

"Christian" who uses their "bully-pulpit" to spread such 'abominable and slanderous' lies that result in the beatings and suicides of so many young and innocent tormented children!

And as I think of the Bible's words: "If anyone says, 'I love God' yet hates his brother, - he is a LIAR!" So I am now forced to wonder if Tony Perkins, by his actions, is not only a biblical liar and a False Christian; but as I'm made un-comfortably aware of his UN-CHRIST-LIKE response to the deaths of so many homosexual children, I wonder if Tony Perkins could also be possibly a narcissist? I question this especially since I know that a narcissist believes that he (or she) is "special" and unique and can only be understood, or should associate with, other special or high-status people. A narcissist shows arrogant, haughty behaviors or attitudes – lacks empathy – and is unwilling to recognize or identify with the feelings and needs of others. And, YES, a "Christian" narcissist is a "Christian" that suffers from extreme self-centeredness.

Plus, as I think of the power of - PROJECTING - I wonder if when Tony Perkins said, "gay teens resort to 'depression or suicide' because – "THEY KNOW THEY'RE 'ABNORMAL'" is Tony Perkins projecting his own "abnormality" onto gay teens? Only a true clinical psychologist can answer those questions and that's for sure.

And Tony Perkins while I may be confused about a lot of things in this world one thing I'm sure of is you, sir, are the kind of person my therapist warned me about staying away from and avoiding and you, sir, could definitely benefit from many hours spent partaking in receiving your own mental health therapy sessions and I for one will, because of your unloving, uncompassionate UNCHRISTIAN actions, pray for YOUR amoral, IMMORTAL SOUL! And I "challenge" you, sir, do go and get some True Counseling before you decide to "beat up" on any more vulnerable teenage children! And I'm even willing to ask you, PLEASE SIR, go get some serious psychological help, if not for your own soul's sake - at least do it for the LOVE OF GOD!

And Tony Perkins if you are going to "quote the Bible" please personally meditate long and deeply on 2 Peter 3:15-16

"Bear in mind that our Lord's patience means salvation, just as our dear brother Paul also wrote you with the wisdom that God gave him. He writes the same way in all his letters, speaking in them of these matters. HIS LETTERS CONTAIN SOME THINGS THAT

ARE HARD TO UNDERSTAND, WHICH - IGNORANT AND UNSTABLE PEOPLE DISTORT, - AS THEY DO THE OTHER SCRIPTURES, - TO THEIR OWN DESTRUCTION!"

And in finishing this very important chapter…. All I can think of now is to say, "Yes, when Tony Perkins and all of his "Day of Truth" Christians do meet Jesus face to face they may ALL have even more of a – CHALLENGING TIME – explaining to Jesus why their Christian mouths didn't match up with their UN-Christian ACTIONS!

And now in spite of all of the hate they direct toward all of us, who are homosexual, I will now pray…. "Heavenly Father, please forgive their very "IGNORANT AND UNSTABLE" ways, for they definitely know NOT what they DO when they distort Christ's message of unconditional love!"

Yes, dear Father they know not what they do or what is so obviously printed on page 566 of the N.I.V. Holy Bible - as Jesus himself says, in the "Seven Woes" contained in Matthew 23:15 "Woe to you, - teachers of the law - and Pharisees, you hypocrites! You travel over land and sea to win a single convert, and when he becomes one, - YOU MAKE HIM TWICE AS MUCH A SON OF HELL AS YOU ARE."

And that is, I believe, - the gospel truth!

So as I dwell on the Bible's promise that all of mankind's sins will be forgiven but the sins committed against the Holy Spirit will not, I wonder if religious zealots realize that while they may have the power to take away my legal rights, my freedoms, and even my very life… the one thing they can't ever take away from me is my Holy Spirit. The Holy Spirit is a gift from God and that gift is a gift that is FREELY GIVEN to all who believe. And I DO BELIEVE God loves me even if other "Christians" don't or won't "choose" to now extend God's unconditional Spirit of Love!

THREE TIMES DENIED

So as this confounding debate over God, the Holy Bible, and gays has the potential to kick up a hell of a lot of dirt, I wonder, during His crucifixion which form of abuse hurt Jesus the most, what was Jesus aware of the most – the physical pain of his body – or the mental trauma of rejection to the point of death from people that he still even now continues to love? With Jesus' example in the face of crucifixion, is the question I should now be asking of me: How do I still love the abuser while I also try balancing forgiveness while personally standing up to the "Christian bullies" who so righteously promote all of this god-awful religious-based insane abuse?

But I know Jesus came to inspire us and he has inspired me, and by Jesus knowing what was yet to come, knowing he was to be crucified Jesus told us that three times before the rooster crowed he would be denied by someone he very much loved. I've often wondered if each denial was experienced, to him, like a nail driven through his emotionally sensitive heart. I love Jesus because he knew what was set before him and yet he was still able to make it through his crucifixion with such Grace pouring from his soul. For me, just the thought of being around someone with that much to give with no fear of loss, can you imagine? I now can! Jesus knew that God was within him. Jesus has the Holy Spirit, he was never alone. Jesus went through his crucifixion with God's love and support sustaining and resurrecting His caring Spirit.

So in God's wisdom, equal experiences can lead to equal understandings; and because Jesus knows what it is like to be personally abandoned and crucified, I know he identifies with anyone else who has also been inhumanly rejected or physically abused. Jesus does NOT relate to those who "choose to abuse!" This gives me comfort knowing he can relate to me on the occasions I've been cast off and cursed. I know Jesus identifies with us in our worldly pain and suffering so the only way to stop Jesus from feeling more pain is to make sure that we never inflict pain - upon even those the world classifies as of low stature. For Jesus Himself said, "What you do to the lowest of the low, that very thing – you continue to do to me."

I love Jesus' thoughts of comfort. Those words tell me Jesus continues to be with us all from the most important to the least of us - we are all important and loved equally as a Holy One through the eyes of Christ.

But in this contentious war weary world, as I try to find my center with Christ at the heart of it all,

I read that gays are WRONG - WRONG – WRONG!

This Op .ed. article was printed in the Daily Oklahoman Newspaper on Sunday, March 16th 2008. The article was printed in the "Your Views" section. It was submitted by Diane Habersaat as her response to all the verbal sparring over who is right about what is wrong in the hotly argued Holy War against Homosexuals!

"Thank God for State Rep. Sally Kern, who had the courage to tell the truth about the "Homosexual agenda" Richard Ogden of Cimarron Alliance said, "This is about responsibility and accountability for words, not freedom of expression." WRONG!

Kern has every right under our Constitution to say exactly what she did and more. Do the homosexuals want to be silenced for all their hate letters and death threats (speaking of terrorism)? State Rep. Al Lindley said that those in the Legislature who are not themselves homophobic "are intimidated by a vocal faction who are." WRONG!

The people are being intimidated and terrorized by all the "Gay Rights" groups who are pushing to get hate crimes legislation passed whereby our freedom of speech will be silenced along with our ability to preach the truth from God's word. According to "Clipped: Lawmaker's stance not a surprise" (Our Views, March 12th) Kern's remarks were "callous and wrong" and she would be better off not "engaging in ideological combat." WRONG! It's about time someone had enough guts to stand up to the "ideological combat" that the homosexual community has been waging against the very fabric of American society."

Diane Habersaat, Oklahoma City

Now, I know we are in a State of War, and war is hell, but that letter the first time I read it was like a bomb shell going off in my head piercing through to my heart! The words in Diane's letter emphasizing WRONG – WRONG –WRONG each pounding pronouncement of WRONG, each and every piercing WRONG, pummeled "the very fabric of my soul."

So, I confess, I've been in a homosexual's mental-abuse recovery program and it's taken me quite a few years to heal my heart and soul enough to try to continue fighting on… but now that I'm feeling a little better and a little stronger, I would like to personally address you Diane - as one fellow Christian to another.

Dear Diane Habersaat,

With all due respect, I don't know you as a person and I know that you don't know me. So to start off the introduction, I hope you will allow me the necessary Grace to claim Christ as my savior!

I'm so very sorry that you feel the way you do about the "homosexual agenda" but I also know you are not alone in the way you feel. There are many people who feel that not only can gays NOT be saved but, directly to the point, some people feel that homosexuals are actively fighting against the Kingdom of God. Being an Evangelical Christian myself, I've personally talked to many other Christians who feel that homosexuals are in league with Satan himself. I was even, once or twice, directly told to my face that with me being openly gay - I was no better than the god-damned devil.

Yes, they even told me to my face that I was also "anti-family!" But Diane, claiming to be a Christian - my own mother turned her back to me and abandoned me when I was honest to her about my sexuality. I haven't heard from my own mother in over 30 years, not one word of encouragement not one word of care. So, in all honesty, what really confuses me about being gay is not my sexuality but - what's God's definition of "family values" - more to the heart of it: What's God's definition of "True Christian-behavior?"

I know in this world many people honor blood lines and consider only "DNA" as the proper and respectable family to value but - what about God's family? Diane, what about God's all inclusive family? More importantly, Diane, what if you are the one WRONG and God still calls me His Child?

Yes, I am gay and, yes, I am a Christian! I Love God, I worship Jesus, and just as important – I read my Holy Bible. And this is where I am most confused about family values!

Growing up I was temporarily adopted many times by many different families. It was stressful growing up that way but now I thank God I was able to meet and inter-react with a lot of different sets of personalities. Some people were good and some were definitely bad. And then there were the True Christians who taught me through their actions what it means to care about someone else. Diane, we all like to care about someone else, that's what makes us feel good inside, the problem is that too often we let judgments get in the way of allowing us to love, we have expectations we have so many conditions.

Every different family I lived with had different pet sins and trespasses and every different family I lived with had very different sins that were punished for being against their individual traditional family values. With some families when your sin was judged bad enough they said you were no longer to be loved! They would instead say "just go away, you are not welcome here anymore."

I guess some people just don't want to value forgiveness. Or, maybe they just don't want to value the power of an education that may help us all to be able to stop obsessing about the sins we think we see other people make? I do know there are many different sins that offend and repulse the many different families of the world. So Diane, if you are bound and determined to so harshly judge homosexuals, how well do you know me as a gay Evangelical Christian? How many people, with different rules and regulations, do you think I was exposed to by living with six different families in four different cities as I went to four different high schools in two different states during just four traumatic years of my life?

Only God knows - and that's why I love Him so much!

Diane, some of the families in my past temporarily took care of me because they knew I didn't have anywhere else to go. These days while a lot of people talk about traditional family values, I confess - the only value I learned to respect was the value of someone else's unconditional love!

For me growing up was hard enough with no true stability but compound that with being unacceptably gay and you will have a rocky journey ahead of you. I did! But God IS a loving Father and He saw to it that I was taken care of while Jesus healed my bumps, broken heart, and many inner bruises. Jesus has also taught me many great lessons about what is to be considered a real tender love!

To this day, I will always remember the "family members" that stood out to me by them letting me know that I was someone they valued and, even if I was gay, they valued thinking good thoughts about me they valued having me around. And so I have to thank Jesus that by his true followers' examples and by his true followers embracing me Jesus, through them, showed me that I will always be a valued member of his family. Yes, I'm definitely a part of Jesus' family who now just wants to extend God's grace and mercy.

And I thank you Jesus, for all of the different people in the very different homes of the many different and diverse faiths who I was exposed to and who ultimately showed me what real love is by their willingness to take care of the cast off children of the world. I now know - I have been adopted by a God who has many wonderful and religiously diverse followers capable of understanding love beyond the mere physical and mental limitations of only valuing that worldly image of "the totally perfect family."

So Yes, Diane, I'm very sorry for the both of us that you don't feel like I, as a homosexual, deserve to be a very natural part of your extended family. I will still say, God bless you and your chosen family whomever you choose to honor with that title. But I'm still very sad for all of us because it seems like Satan, so often, is so easily able to keep us all from respecting each other equally, in great amounts.... one to the other.

This letter is sincerely written to you with best future wishes, including the deep desire that our whole world will one day "awaken" to the true love of God, and yes, I'm an out and proud..... fellow seeker of Salvation

So Who is Right About What is WRONG?

This is right and that is wrong! That is wrong and this is right! Back and forth the extreme shouts and screams shoot by us. In this deranged Holy War against Homosexuals few are questioning the necessity OF war while many seem to be questioning only the constitutionality or the morality of the many divisive issues. So who is right when both sides seem to want to fight and the only one who comes out ahead in a Holy War is Satan?

Does it all come down to interpretations? Like two versions of the same person is it all a matter of whom you ask? Hero or villain, sinner or saint, are they False Christians or are those people the True?

And what of a parable told to us by Jesus, which do we choose to believe when now it is discovered to be not just simply one parable but a very distinctly, different two? With dark and light, love and hate, will the answer be found between the shadings – the extreme contrasts in Christians... this is what we're now debating. Beauty IS in the eye of the beholder while the beholder chooses to see the evil or the sublime beauty!

The Parable of the Weeds

Jesus told them the kingdom of heaven is like a man who sowed good seeds in his field. But while everyone was sleeping his enemy came and sowed weeds among the wheat and went away. When the wheat sprouted and formed heads, then the weeds also appeared. The owner's servants came to him and said, "Sir, didn't you sow good seed in your field? Where did the weeds come from?" "An enemy did this" he replied. The servants asked him, "Do you want us to go and pull them up?" "No" he answered, "because while you are pulling the weeds, you may root up the wheat with them. Let both grow together until the harvest. At that time I will tell the harvesters; first collect the weeds and then tie them in bundles to be burned; then gather the wheat and bring it into my barn."

To a traditionally fundamentalist evangelical Christian this parable is simply talking about good people versus bad people and how God will eventually separate the good people from the bad people – bad people will then burn in hell while the good people of the world get to go to heaven. I know this parable interpretation has been used to justify condemning many a person to a future hell while it has also been used to justify making too many a person's life on earth a present hell!

But with me being gay, a casualty of war, and being cast out from the embraces of the Southern Baptist Church I have still fought on with continuing my spiritual quest and I am now in possession of a different more loving Grace filled explanation for the parable of the weeds.

With interpretation number two, I have been told the parable of the weeds is a promise of salvation for all – it's totally the opposite from a warning of hell and evangelical damnation! With this new and more enlightened interpretation: Words are seeds and some words help us to love while some words germinate hate! With re-thinking the Parable of the Weeds, the field is the Holy Bible and the enemy is Satan. In the darkness of God's Children falling asleep the Holy Bible was contaminated by the seeds of Satan and his army of False Apostle Christians. They planted shady seeds of bad thoughts that can cause internal divisions and separations amongst all of God's good Children. So upon awakening and reading the Holy Bible while digesting its contents of many different words some of God's Children become very loving while some of God's Children become very judgmental. These False Christian worshiping children have decided to make war a holy hell kind of religious nightmare for everyone. But, mercifully, because God doesn't ever want to lose ANY of His Children – no matter how badly they might misunderstand the Bible or misbehave at the polls - He has told the Angels to wait until the time of harvest when His Children have all fully grown up in maturity, education, and in love, at

30

that time of spiritual re-birth God's Children will be wise enough and compassionate enough to go back and reread and rethink the Bible's message of hope and redemption. Then, with God's merciful promise, they will be able to save themselves by each individual child giving to all the other children all good grace. Then all of God's good Children will be finally freed from the lies of the deceiver. One of those sinful lies is Satan's core lie that God is very judgmental. Satan also wants us to believe that God doesn't want to love or is powerless to save all of His many different Children! These tragic False Christian lies are the only "bundles of bad thoughts" deserving of forever now burning. And once we all finally do burn off all of those weedy false lies... That's what will return us all to our rightful place of inward heavenly bliss.

Yes, I remember how blissful I was the first time I realized I had been lied to by Satan – NO – I wasn't alone in this world. What a natural high, such a good feeling! Not to be or feel alone.... And not just the time I realized I wasn't the only "normal homosexual" – I remember the time I was exposed to the anti-lie fact that there are many more out there that are like me. I am like they are. We may be "in the loving minority," but we are the same and we are one. We believe that God's Grace will eventually save everybody, like yeast slowly working itself through the kneaded dough – A Christ-like love will eventually win out over all of Satan's hate even with all of our present day heartaches with those people projecting so much inner-hell and self-damnation!"

So in appreciation of being given a huge amount of grace to counter-act my huge heartache over the issues of fighting off all of those fearful False Christian lies, "If Grace is True" isn't just a concept for us to now intelligently discuss, it's a book!

"If Grace Is True" Why God will save every person, is a book co-written by Philip Gulley and James Mulholland.

The book captured my battle weary soul when it explained: "Why Everyone Will Be In Heaven. Two pastors present their controversial belief in eternal salvation for all through God's perfect grace. Long disturbed by the Church's struggle between offering both love and rejection, they discover what God wants from us and for us: grace for everyone."

And as I read their book I have to wonder, are we marching through the eye of the proverbial needle finally on our way to understanding

Heaven? Narrow is the road that leads to Heaven, and that Heaven can only be reached by Grace and Grace is a double-edged sword because we can only receive as much Grace for ourselves as the amount of Grace we are freely willing to now extend? So as we willfully, purposefully extend....

According to Philip Gulley and James Mulholland, "My experience is not unique. Many testify to the power of the Jesus story. In ways we don't fully understand and can't completely communicate, we were drawn to Jesus. And yet not to Jesus alone. It was the God of Jesus that attracted us. The God who loves people more than formulas, mercy more than judgment, and pardon more than punishment. The God who seeks the lost, heals the brokenhearted, accepts the outcast, is kind to the wicked and ungrateful, is merciful and forgiving, and loves the whole world.

Now I realize there are many hindrances to experiencing the fullness of God's grace – confusion, fear, prejudice, ignorance, and pride to name a few. The removal of these obstacles ought to be the primary purpose of the Church. Unfortunately, the Church has often erected more barriers than we've removed. Too many have entered our doors, only to experience condemnation rather than welcome. We've acted less like Jesus and more like his opponents."

And of course I am personally awed when they write, "Many, like me, have experienced God's love but have misunderstood salvation. We've thought it a trophy rather than a gift, a personal achievement rather than a work of God. We've gloried in our own salvation and damned those whose obstacles have far exceeded our own."

And with me being a gay male Evangelical Christian who has been deeply hurt by the traditional Church, as I read the words of Philip Gulley, a Quaker minister and James Mulholland an American Baptist, I find that Jesus - through all of their combined words – is healing the many inner wounds to my soul. And I understand forgiveness on a deeper level than ever before.

And as a gay Christian how can I say how much I respect their total honestly when they write, "Ironically, both the rejected and the righteous have misunderstood the grace of God. The rejected assume their "sinful" behavior has removed them from God's affection and desire. The righteous conclude their "goodness" has assured them god's love and favor. Both groups have defined their relationship with God by their behavior rather than by God's character and will. In that sense, both groups are self-absorbed."

I loved it when they write, "I discovered the meaning of salvation. Salvation comes with believing God loves you unconditionally. It is abandoning the misconception that you are rejected because of your bad behavior or accepted because of your goodness. Only when we repent of this self-absorption and focus on God's love can this love alter us. Then and only then can God transform hearts darkened by sin and soften hearts hardened by self-righteousness.

It is from this self-absorption that we must be saved. Often, when I speak of my belief in the salvation of every person, someone will object that without the threat of hell, people would sin wantonly. They consider the possibility of eternal punishment as the only deterrent to human selfishness. Unfortunately, if this is true, even serving God and loving our neighbor becomes acts of selfishness. Self-absorbed choices, by their very nature, separate us from God and from others. I learned this from Jesus."

And now, thank God, I can say I have learned of all of this from Philip Gulley and James Mulholland.

But then as the sounds of war once again comes crashing down all around me I read, "I was raised to believe homosexuals were sexual perverts and child molesters. They were the worst of sinners and doomed for hell. I accepted this belief uncritically and, since I knew no homosexuals, found that belief easy to sustain."

But by the grace of God, a willingness to learn, and a multiple of years spent in a conversion of experience, further on I read in "If Grace Is True,"….. "God spent fifteen years chiseling away at my stone beliefs and softening the hardened clay of my heart. I try to be gentle when I share my new beliefs about homosexuality with those who were taught what I once believed. I realize that if I had not had a close friend who was a Christian and a homosexual I probably would never have changed my belief. Experience is a powerful teacher."

Then, for me, like the Calvary coming to the rescue, at a critical point in time I also read, "I remember my dismay when early in the AIDS crisis many Christian leaders explained AIDS as a punishment from God. Some seemed to find great satisfaction, even joy, in the slow and painful death of homosexuals. One of my first funerals as a pastor was for a young man who died of AIDS. His family told no one of his death and invited no one to his brief graveside service. After the funeral, his father grieved that he had failed his son. A year later, I would officiate at his funeral after he took a gun and killed himself.

Let me be perfectly clear. I no longer want anything to do with a god who punishes homosexuals by giving them a terrible disease. I want nothing to do with a god who murders children in order to maintain racial purity. I cannot believe in a god who will eternally punish a vast majority of his children. This isn't the God of Jesus. This isn't the God I have experienced. It is certainly not a god I can worship."

So thankfully, like a healing balm, the words of Philip Gulley and James Mulholland refresh my beaten down spirit and I think I am finally starting to see what the words – to see Christ in another human being – truly means!

But now a shock wave knocks me over as I wonder again, who is the False Christian and who is the True?

And as the battle over "what's right and who's right" rages on, I read again from, "If Grace Is True."

"Many decide to escape the pain of growth by uncritically adopting the beliefs they were taught. One of the most discouraging responses I've received to my belief in the salvation of every person has been, "Well, that sounds good, but I've believed since I was a child that some people will go to heaven and some will go to hell. Don't ask me to change my mind now." They then proceed to quote certain Scriptures that support what they were taught as a child. I listen politely, since I was taught these same verses. I freely admit to them that my belief is contrary to certain Scriptures. Then I cite other Scriptures that have often been ignored. They frequently scratch their heads in befuddlement. Some even ask, "If the Bible says two different things, how do we know which is true?"

And then a couple of concepts explodes from within me: Perhaps if I'm not the only one who personally thinks the Bible says two different things at two different times then, with double-vision, adding the fact that one parable can have two contrasting interpretations, then I think this is all for me concrete proof that any damning kind of quote or parable interpretation could just be another Satanic-try-at-deception just to get us to keep-on fighting-on, cursing one another!

So now for me, with this inner battle finally coming to a rest, the Parable of the Weeds with interpretation number two is the True Way to interpret the parable. And, for me, after mentally regrouping and reprocessing all of these new and lovingly anti-traditional thoughts I become even more convinced that Satan and his False Christian prophets really have, deep in the past, contaminated the Holy Bible by sowing in seeds of damnation and discontent by playing off our perceptions and our ability to always see things in two-distinct-ways. And now thanks to Satan's weeds of double-crossing-vision and standards, we will always have a reason to see something wrong with someone else and proudly quote one Scripture, or its contrasting Scripture, while egging on one hellacious fight.

But doesn't all of this Christian conflict tell me that if I'm ever discontent and damn any of my fellow family in Christ… doesn't that really tell me in truth I have been blind? Or, is the correct interpretation: I have been blinded-by Satan's hate?

But once again I am suddenly perplexed because even to be blind can also be a theoretical double-edged sword – The curse of the Lord or a blessing sent from God? Yet, I truly see, I can choose to be blind to God's love of extending free grace – or I can forevermore now choose just to be blind to the False Christian concept of eternally damning "mortal-sin"!

And with all of these complex battles now being fought around me and still being debated within me, I have to really try and focus my sight but even with all of my new found hope all I can really see clearly right now is that things are, for me, very possibly raging toward total Christian insanity as I wonder - at the world - and myself, am I getting better or worse, am I on the right tract or have I just hit a salvation snag? I do know the hardest battle yet still to be fought is the concept about the majority of the Christian world as being so wrong… about so many things…. for far too long!

While I know most people believe in hell for punishment I just know it makes me think so much more highly of God the Father as when I think of Him as being a loving, patient, in control Father, yes, when I think of Him as never ever throwing His Own Children, discarded, out with the trash - no matter how bad someone's negative ideology might stink!

And then, after realizing just how bad Satan wants us to condemn each other to hell while we're quoting our favorite choices of the Bible's contrasting Scriptures, it hits me that instead of continuing "the normal tradition" of separating people from one another.... maybe the really wise ones just need to separate the F.C. mental B.S. from the Blessed Truth!

Therefore to focus on finding the blessed truth, I thank God that he put a very important book directly into my soul searching hands called, "IF GRACE IS TRUE!" And I rejoice that - if grace IS true – it's now, for me, no longer just a theoretical question for me to constantly wrestle with but instead... it's a concept strongly supported by a very good book's teachings all set around God's Ever-Inclusive Grace!

THE FREEDOM TO GAY-BASH

On Sunday April 23rd 2006 in the continuing Holy War against Homosexuals I read an eye-opening news piece by Christopher Curtis of PlanetOut, he writes: "Students sue to protect anti-gay speech"

"Three Pennsylvania high schoolers have sued the Downington Area School District after it prevented them from expressing their views on the "sinful nature and harmful effects of homosexuality." Stephanie Styler, Steven Styler and Kim Kowalsky want to express at school their belief "that there is a superior religious point of view to other competing views that would, for example, affirm a homosexual lifestyle."

"High schools in America are not enclaves of totalitarianism," their federal lawsuit states. "Through its written policies and action, [the district] is violating the free speech and associational rights of every student on its campus." Attorneys for the three students believe they will prevail, since the wording of the district's anti-harassment policy resembles one from the State College Area School District that the 3rd Circuit U.S. Court of Appeals struck down five years ago.

Judge Samuel Alito Jr., who has since been elevated to the U.S. Supreme Court, wrote: "The Supreme Court has held time and again, both within and outside of the school context, that the mere fact that someone might take offense at the content of speech is not sufficient justification for prohibiting it."

It's at this point in my reading that I get confused over all these complex issues again, so I wonder about "it", is "it" about not prohibiting anti-gay content of speech or is Samuel Alito saying, "the mere fact that someone might take offense at the content of speech is not sufficient justification for prohibiting homosexuality?"

I wonder especially because all physical actions can only be legally conveyed by words used to ultimately describe the actions-taken and acceptance or offense are also seen as different and competing views over words or action; so staring my own confusion in the face, I press on with my deep questioning of life, love, and the True or is it a False Christian agenda? I read more of Christopher Curtis' article:

"The Pennsylvania law suit is part of a broader effort by the Alliance Defense Fund, a right-wing legal group that works nationwide to attack anti-harassment policies that protect LGBT students.

Last month, the Alliance Defense Fund filed suit on behalf of Georgia Tech senior Ruth Malhotra and junior Orit Sklar, claiming the students fear they may be punished for violating the school's conduct guidelines in expressing anti-gay sentiments. The Alliance Defense Fund calls such policies illegal "speech codes" that violate the First Amendment.

It was dealt a setback Thursday, however, when the 9th Circuit of the U.S. Court of Appeals refused Thursday to approve a preliminary injunction against a suburban San Diego high school that pulled a sophomore from class for sporting a shirt that read: "Be Ashamed, Our School Embraced What God has "Condemned" and "Homosexuality is Shameful, Romans 1:27"

The 9th Circuit panel compared the shirt's impact of LGBT students with the effect of a swastika or a Confederate flag on Jewish or black students, and said the school had no obligation to "provide equal time for... speech espousing intolerance, bigotry, or hatred."

"There is a national problem with suppressing free speech at high schools and colleges in the name of political correctness, and it disproportionally affects conservative and Christian students and student organizations," David French, director of the group's Center for Academic Freedom, told the Philadelphia Inquirer.

"The educational establishment thinks it has figured out the answers to the burning social questions and the answers are almost always on the left side of the spectrum and counter to traditional Judeo-Christian values, which are labeled as intolerant, harassing, and bigoted." French said.

And yet, for me, in spite of the fact that everyone involved with this legal issue is on different ends of the polarity fighting to get their own views heard, after reading all of this, I still think of how well I can relate to those kids promoting the anti-gay lawsuit. Yes, I think to myself – how many times have I also wondered if I'm going to be severely punished for what I do too? Being a gay Evangelical, I totally understand what the fear and threat of punishment will do to your peace and stability of mind!

But I also wonder, in legal code, does "the students fear they may be punished for violating the school's conduct guidelines in expressing anti-gay sentiments" does this just translate that the kids at some point crossed the line from verbal hate speech to physical hate action? Or is it like my therapist has taught me, mental abuse is just as destructive to a person as physical abuse and so, logically, do those kids fear punishment from the school district for them being blatant public religious bullies? Or really on a deeper level, for so many of us, does it all burn down to the fact that everyone always seems to be so afraid we're all going to end up in hell - strictly to receive the ultimate in punishment from God?

I know I was once afraid of not just punishment but also I feared the wrath and scorn of God, I was deathly afraid of hell. They told me in church to, "Fear the Lord!" Yes, as my knees quaked in my pew the Cultural Warriors have promised me I'll suffer eternal torment in hell, but then in reading my Bible, I get reaffirmed that God is love. 1 john 4:16-17

"God is love. Whoever lives in love lives in God, and God in him. In this way, love is complete among us so that we will have confidence on the day of judgment because in this world we are like him........ there is no fear in love.

And that's where doing a little research for my own salvation has paid off! This contrast of views over the concept of punishment and how a True Christian should view the use of "punishment" is found in the Bible, 1 John 4:18

"There is no fear in love. But perfect love drives out fear, because fear has to do with punishment. The one who fears is not made perfect in love."

And again, thank God for logic and reasoning, so if God IS perfect love then that statement tells me God never embraces punishment of any form - for any reason. But, I debate, as long as Christians "fear" homosexuals will they NEVER ever be able to relate to... "perfect-love?" Then everything seems to confound me once again as I read on May 7th 2009 terribly disturbing news. This war related article is written by Leonard Pitts Jr. and was distributed by the Miami Herald. "Commentary: Why do we tolerate torture?"

"Between 1933 and 1945, as a serried of restrictive laws, brutal pogroms and mass deportations culminating in the slaughter of six million Jews, the Christian church, with isolated exceptions, watched in silence.

Between 1955 and 1968, as forces of oppression used terrorist bombings, police violence and kangaroo courts to deny African Americans their freedom, the Christian church, with isolated exceptions watched in silence.

Beginning in 1980, as a mysterious and deadly new disease called AIDS began to rage through the homosexual community like an unchecked fire, the Christian church, with isolated exceptions, watched in silence.

So who can be surprised by the new Pew report?

Specifically, it's from the Pew Research Center's Forum on Religion & Public Life, and it surveys Americans' attitudes on the torture of suspected terrorists. Pew found that 49 percent of the nation believes torture is at least sometimes justifiable. Slice that number by religious affiliation, though, and things get interesting. It turns out the religiously unaffected are the least likely (40 percent) to support torture, but that the more you attend church, the more likely you are to condone it. Among racial/religious groups, white evangelical Protestants were far and away the most likely (62 percent) to support inflicting pain as a tool of interrogation.

You'd think people who claim connection to a higher morality would be the ones most likely to take the lonely, principled stand. But you need only look at history to see how seldom that has been the case, how frequently my people – Christians – acquiesce to expediency and fail to look beyond the immediate. Never mind that looking beyond the immediate pretty much constitutes a Christian's entire job description.

In the Bible it says, "Perfect loves casts out fear." What we see so often in people of faith, though, is an imperfect love that embraces fear, that lets us live contentedly in our moral comfort zones, doing spiritual busywork and clucking pieties, things that let you feel good, but never require you to put anything at risk, take a leap, make that lonely stand.

Again, there are exceptions, but they prove the rule, which is that in our smug belief that God is on our side, we often fail to ask if we are on His.

So it is often left to few iconoclasts – Oskar Schindler, the war profiteer who rescued 1,200 Jews in Poland; James Reeb, the Unitarian Universalist minister murdered for supporting African-American voting rights in Alabama; Princess Diana, the British royal who courted international opprobrium for simply touching a person with AIDS in Britian – to do the dangerous and moral thing while the great body of Christiandom watches in silence.

Now there is this ongoing debate over the morality of torture in which putative people of faith say they can live with a little blood (someone else's) and a little pain (also someone else's) if it helps maintain the illusion of security (theirs),and never mind such niceties as guilt or innocence.

Thus it was left to Jon Stewart, the cheerfully irreligious host of The Daily Show, to speak last week of the need to be willingly bound by rules of decency and civilization or else be indistinguishable from the terrorists. "I understand the impulse," he said. "I wanted them to clone bin Laden so that we could kill one a year at half-time at the Super Bowl.... I understand blood-lust, I understand revenge, I understand all those feelings. I also understand that this country is better than me."

So there you have it: A statement of principle and higher morality from a late-night comic. That Christians are not lining up to say the same is glaringly ironic in light of what happened to a Middle Eastern man who was arrested by the government, imprisoned and tortured. Eventually he was even executed, though he was innocent of any crime. His name was Jesus."

And after reading Leonard Pitts' to the heart of it all story, as I question the morality of any "Christian" who would condone any torture for any reason, it regretfully makes sense to me, as a gay white

Bible Belt Christian, because the truth is - I've gone to way too many churches who still adamantly preach, "Spare the rod and spoil the child" and , God does know…. if they have to inflict a little spiritual pain to get someone to confess and convert to their ways – so be it!" So it only makes perfect sense that an imperfect False Christian love will always make sure it has its cherished rod of righteous punishment – always close at hand.

So, while I dwell on the use of "Christian torture" and Sally Kern's recommendation that, "When people lack inner-restraints you have to rely upon outer-restraints to control them" and while I'm once again reminded of Cultural Warriors and those Christians quick to pick a fight - as these conceptual battles rage on, I think of not just punishment for sins but also judgment, what of all of the talk of the "day of judgment"? Is there really, for us, a day of judgment and if there is - who really judges who? I have to admit I only wish, in this world, I could hear the pulpit words, "God loves you unconditionally" as often as so many of us have all heard the words, "God will judge you most assuredly!"

So I get more confused because I know God didn't send Jesus to judge, Jesus came to save. I do believe that above it all, but I also read the most important words of Jesus in the Bible, John 5:22 "Because, the Father judges no one but has entrusted all judgment to the Son."

And adding, John 8:15 Jesus said, "You judge by human standards, I pass judgment on no one." And again, John 12:47 "I do not judge him for I did not come to judge the world but to save it." When I add all of these words from Jesus together I get the concept that "the Father judges no one, and Jesus passes judgment on no one, so… if God doesn't judge and Jesus doesn't judge that tells me, "I should also NEVER ever judge if I want to be a true Christian!" And I do want to be a true Christian! But then I'm kicked with the thought, "if Cultural Warriors judge me can they really be True Christians?" God only knows….

But still I wonder, now that the Bible plainly tells me I won't be judged by God or Jesus, so… on that promised evangelical Day of Judgment will those people who have just gotten so into the habit of judgment, in truth, will they really just end up only being able to judge their own personal self when they first find themselves standing next to a person who can love and forgive more than they can? With me now learning the false from the true is judgment nothing more than the contrast we find between different people being a truly loving accepting Christian versus being a truly ungrateful Christian who willingly and proudly condemns others? And then, in my heart with all of this new knowledge, I take a pledge to get much better at forgiving those who love to persecute me, while I'm definitely trying my damndest at losing – in my heart… the "legal right" Satan lets us all feel free to use while pointing the finger at anyone for any reason.

But, I do sometimes think of all of the times I've been personally condemned and warned of hell as my due punishment and I contrast it with the words found in the Bible; yes, when I seek for it the Bible tells me to forgive and that God and Jesus WILL NOT stand in judgment of me. And then I think of all of the churches in the world that now proudly pray to God while they are still continuing to preach hatred toward me for being who I honestly am. Yet I know the Bible also says, 1 John 3:15

"Anyone who hates his brother is a murderer and you know that no murderer has eternal life in him."

Yet by many churches I am judged and I am hated as a homosexual. So I do wonder what they who condemn my sexual orientation will say on that day when Jesus finally does ask them, "Why?" Why can't they ever forgive homosexuals? Why won't they stop standing in such harsh judgment? Why wouldn't they forgive homosexuals even when it means their own sins could have been forgiven too? And "could have been forgiven" are these the operative words because by the time we do meet Jesus will it be too late to learn how to unconditionally forgive? Only Jesus knows for sure.…

But for me, even while I'm still caught up in this terribly confusing Holy War against Homosexuals I must always remember the words found in Mark 11:25

"And when you stand praying if you hold anything against anyone, forgive him, so that your Father in heaven may forgive you your sins."

So for me, that's going to be one of the hardest parts – for me to now forgive those Christians who feel they need to fight for the legal right to protect the freedom to gay-bash till their torturing hearts are content! Yes, all this and more do they legally demand – yet without ever wanting to have to fear for their very own safety or punishment and I think, my God, how ironic!

And then I think... Oh, what a tangled web we weave when first Satan convinces us of our naturally "superior religious point of view to other competing points of view that would, for example, affirm" – to judge not lest ye be FOUND FALSE?

Then I find a well of anger is starting to gush up from deep inside of me as the words from the Holy Bible flash ever-stronger straight at me, 1 Corinthians 6:4-8

"Therefore, if you have disputes about such matters, appoint as judges even men of little account in the church! I say this to shame you. Is it possible that there is nobody among you wise enough to judge a dispute between believers? But instead, one brother goes to law against another – and this in front of unbelievers! The very fact that you have law suits among you means you have been completely defeated already. Why not rather be wronged? Why not rather be cheated? Instead, you yourselves cheat and do wrong, and this you do to your brothers. "

And thinking about all of the atheists who have now been blinded to God's love by all this False Christian legal wrangling now going on... and on... and on... realizing that when it does come down to reading Jesus' holy words found in red knowing that in the Bible Jesus NEVER said anything against homosexuals while he did mention many times the dangers of hypocrisy... so I do know that when my time comes and I do see Jesus eye to eye – I'm darn sure I would rather have him call me a homosexual than to have Him call me a self-blind hypocrite! Then I wonder how the un-loving parts of the straight world would react if all homosexuals wore a t-shirt that said, "Beware the sinful nature and harmful effects of Christian hypocrisy!"? So, to contrast, instead of kids saying, "That's so gay," maybe in reality, "That's so damn hypocritical," and with that very serious thought I'm afraid I'm going a little crazier as I realize how much some Christians hate me for not following - Biblical law - when they sure don't seem to be guided by the "straight letter" of "the law" either!

But it's here I again thank God for all of my therapy sessions because with that last set of soul damaging hypocritical thoughts, I realized that anger flowing up from inside of me is just letting Satan tempt me into being mean spirited and bitter – and so I repent and I focus instead on all of the love I've been given instead.... And I pray the love I HAVE been given wells up from deep inside of me and cancels out all of the negative... and hurtful... and abusive thoughts... it's so easy for so many of us to continue to use.

And dear God, no matter how many people Stephanie, Steven, Kim, Ruth, or Orit, - intentionally or unintentionally - hurt while publically pointing out the sins of only others, please bless them and shower them with Your Overflowing Unconditional Love...... then maybe one day by experiencing the abundance of Your True Love those kids, and many other kids just like them, will finally radiate that same fullness of pure sweet-love to all others.

A CONDEMNING LETTER

This is natural, this is very unnatural, doing this will get you into heaven, but doing this will drive you straight to hell.....

And as the continuing Holy War against Homosexuals heats up another notch, I read a news flash sent by Christopher Curtis of PlanetOut.Network, he writes:

"The president of the U.S. Conference of Catholic Bishops wants all Roman Catholics to oppose marriage between same-sex couples by supporting a federal constitutional amendment that would ban it. "Today there is a growing sense shared by many people, including a wide range of religious leaders, that a marriage protection amendment is the only federal-level action that ultimately will protect and preserve the institution of marriage," Bishop William Skylstad wrote in a letter dated March 27th and made public Monday.

Skystad wrote that he expected the Protection of Marriage Amendment to be introduced in the Senate in June. "In a matter of months we will have the opportunity once again to stand in support of marriage as the God-given union of a man and a woman," he wrote. "I am aware that the time is short for taking action, so I urge you to do whatever you can, given the situation and resources available to you," Skystad wrote, noting that the Knights of Columbus have initiated a national postcard campaign to support anti-gay legislation.

"I am also aware that in some states there are upcoming votes for either legislation or constitutional amendments defining marriage," Skystad added, "We are challenged, therefore, to give attention to the interplay of state-and federal-level policy as well as to focus our efforts where they are most needed and can do the most good."

Jeremy Learning, spokesman for Americans United for the Separation of Church and State, took issue with Skylstad's proposal.

"I think this confirms what our organization has been arguing for a long time – that the religious majority in America wants the federal marriage amendment to enshrine their idea of marriage in the Constitution and have it imposed on everyone else, and other religions are rendered second class in essence," Learning said.

"We have a constitution that mandates a separation of church and state, and we have these people trying to enshrine their religious views in that very document" he said.

Finally after reading all of this I shake my head and think, "That's all very condemning!"

And my general confusion over condemnation is multiplied ten-fold while I wonder in Jesus' eyes who will really be condemned – gays for wanting a bond of love? Or, in Jesus' eyes will the Catholic Church one day be condemned for publically condemning homosexual love? I have comfort Jesus knows what's up with our Catholic Caesar and that's for sure.

So all this I battle with as I'm again reminded of the words found in Jesus' prayer, "Father, forgive us as we forgive those".... who now just want to get married? Or, dear God, do we also need to forgive those who just want to abolish us from "the right" to get "legally" married? And as I fight with the knowledge that selfish Christians CAN stop homosexuals from getting "legally married" – in truth they CAN'T stop God Himself from honoring our love; while, within me, the Holy Spirit's answer to all of this worldly fighting is simply, "Just forgive – it doesn't matter which side you have to forgive – in the Spirit of love, just forgive, God knows even if it's only for your own soul's sake – try to forgive!"

But while I try to forgive I still fight with the idea that for some people protecting the sanctity of marriage is of more importance than protecting the sanctity of non-judgment. And I do wonder, what about the sanctity of equality and fair justice? What about protecting the sanctity of sharing good things with others? Soon I'm wrapped up in the idea that Satan's hate has the power to turn us all very egotistical and self-centered as Colossians 2:8 comes into mind, "See to it that no one takes you captive through hollow and deceptive philosophy which depends on human tradition and the basic principles of this world rather than on Christ."

And counter punching that thought, 1 John 3:16-18 "This is how we know what love is: Jesus Christ laid down his life for us, and we ought to lay down our lives for our brothers. If anyone has material possessions and see his brother in need but has no pity on him, how can the love of God be in him? Dear (True) children, let us not love with words or tongue but with actions and in truth."

And, as I think of all of the Christians who, by their actions, have no pity on homosexuals or see a homosexuals need to get married, then I wonder about all of those sacred straight traditions, as I ask myself, "What's wrong with embracing the sanctity of only their traditions?" Then the battle within my mind gets worse because when I think of the importance of their traditions of old I read for myself what Jesus is supposed to have thought of plain "old traditions!"

I say, what Jesus is supposed to have thought of "old traditions" because I have been exposed to the knowledge found in the Holy Bible, A Course in Miracles, and the Gospel of Judas. Those three books say many, very many of the same things. But according to A Course in Miracles and the Gospel of Judas - Jesus WAS misquoted in the Bible. Plus, if A Course in Miracles along with the Gospel of Judas both speaks of another story of the creation of the physical world and the creation of man, with two-against-one Genesis, it's all making me very conflicted about who do I trust for the truth? So as I continue to explore all of these new concepts I wonder – who is right – who is so spiritually-dead wrong? Or should I really be questioning, to get at the root of this damning problem, which "holy-quote" is to be found lacking love or reason and therefore wrong?

So I ask myself if it's reasonably true that an all powerful God created, like Genesis says, this Satan seduced world with its False Christians and false prophets its share of evil, destruction, and its ability to honor only a marriage between a woman and a man? Or, on the flip side of the perception according to what I have gleaned from A.C.I.M., did we, as the Children of God, use our own God given creative ability to form this physical world for ourselves while we, ourselves, have separated our own selves into different sexes, labels, and functions? And by separating ourselves from one another, by establishing an unequal imperfect love within us, did we create and project the very imperfect world we find all around us? I do know an unequal love is an imperfect love and I don't believe God creates anything imperfect either in spiritual form or in physical function!

But with all of these many different issues now battling for top priority, I have to remember: first things first.... so march back to traditions and who is wrong about the importance of holding on to traditions, more importantly, what does the Bible quote that Jesus thinks of traditions? Mark7:5-9

"So the Pharisees and the teachers of the law asked Jesus, "Why don't your disciples live according to the tradition of the elders instead of eating their food with "unclean" hands?" He (Jesus) replied, "Isaiah was right when he prophesied about you hypocrites, as it is written: "These people honor me with their lips, but their hearts are far from me. They worship me in vain – their teachings are but rules taught by men. You have let go of the commands of God (to love and forgive one another) and are holding on to the traditions of men. And he (Jesus) said to them, "You have a fine way of setting aside the commands of God in order to observe your own traditions...." And so I wonder if Jesus himself right now personally jumped into the middle of all these worldly arguments over the "un-cleanliness" of same-sex marriage would he reply to the Religious Right, as in Acts 10:28....... "But God has shown me that I should not call ANY man impure or unclean!" While Jesus then proceeds to quote the concept of what lies in Hebrews 13:9 "Do not be carried away by all kinds of strange teachings. It is good for our hearts to be strengthened by GRACE, not by ceremonial rituals...." Then with Jesus' final blow would He have to say to the Moral Majority "I'm so astounded by your un-gracious actions and that tells me you clearly don't understand... so now..." 1 Peter 4:9 "Offer hospitality to one another - WITHOUT GRUMBLING!"

But, in my mind, as I try to come to terms with myself over everyone's personal interpretations in Matthew chapter 15 again it jumps at me in red-hot holy print: Jesus replied, "These people honor me with their lips but their hearts are far from me. They worship me in vain – their teachings are but rules taught by men."

And "rules taught by men" this, it seems for me, goes right to the eye of the dissent because if A Course in Miracles and the Gospel of Judas are both right in that the Bible has been "seeded" with mistaken quotes and past miss-information then, logically I have to always ask myself, "WHAT IF – God did NOT create this world and God did NOT make us male and female and what if God did NOT create the institution of marriage between just a male and a female just to null and void it out when we get to heaven?" Is this worldly issue over the sanctity of marriage just a wedge issue Satan is cunningly using to still keep us emotionally separated and constantly in-fighting? And yes, we're all tied-up in a world-wide-fight to establish what constitutes for our collective societies - legally binding basic human rights.

Then, with basic rights in mind, I have to do great personal battle with the idea that if God didn't create them "male and female" and if the sanctity of marriage is just a rule taught by men - then we, as humans, have really gone off the beaten path and many churches have now been taking the totally dead-wrong path by fostering in us the desire to continually beat up on one another's identities and self-perceptions!

And even though the New Testament stresses many times, "do not be afraid" I find myself afraid the Bible is right, as reason, when in Galatians 3:26-28 it says: "You are all Sons of God through faith in Christ Jesus for all of you who were baptized into Christ have clothed yourselves with Christ. There is neither Jew not Greek, slave nor free, male nor female, for you are all one in Christ Jesus."

So, no male or female means also no gay no straight… then when it does come down to the importance of the sanctity of marriage I also read from the Bible: Matthew 20:29-30 (Jesus said) "You are in error because you do not know the Scriptures or the power of God. At the resurrection people will neither marry nor be given in marriage; they will be like the angels in heaven."

And I confess, yes, I'm afraid that I'll eventually have to give up my general sexual identity to enter into heaven; and, I'm really afraid that if we are all one in Christ – in God's eyes neither male nor female – and if at the resurrection there will be no marriage… I'm afraid all of this worldly fighting over the sanctity of marriage; the issue of – gay vs. straight, marriage vs. civil union - this is just another ploy of the devil to get us to condemn one another by what we will approve of! Curse the devil! And now I realize the full extent of the deceiving power of Satan's double-vision because so many gays are now extremely mad at the straights for being so self-absorbed while so many of the straights so often times truly hate the gays for wanting to just simply get married. And I wonder if Satan is now, without any heart, laughing at us ALL very equally – ?

On judging others... Luke 6:37-38 "Do not judge, and you will not be judged – do not condemn and you will not be condemned. Forgive and you will be forgiven. Give and it will be given to you a good measure, pressed down, shaken together and running over will be poured into your lap..... For with the measure you use it will be measured to you."

And coming to my rescue, I read Romans 14:22 "So whatever you believe about these things keep between yourself and God. Blessed is the man who does not condemn himself by what he approves." So, I finally make a big mental break through while also starting to find that my inner-fear is subsiding all because I finally understand that to condemn the Catholic Church because it is officially condemning me – will only condemn me – in the long run. My mantra is now, "What I do comes back to me, what they do will eventually come back to haunt them, for we all will reap as we sow, and dear God, for now and forevermore please help me to sow a deep rooted love for all of mankind in a very gender neutral non sexual respectful way. In fact, please dear God, give me a head start on understanding the True concept of heaven by helping me to see all of my brothers and sisters as just androgynous Angels while on Earth, that way when I finally do make it to heaven I won't freak out when, along with no marriage, there are also no gentlemen's or ladies' rest rooms, or fashion shows, or guy or gal attitudes. Then I find peace, with no guy or gal attitudes no wonder it's considered a True Heaven... it's without ANY False Christian sexually-charged conflict or dissention!

After taking a deep breath, as I quietly reflect on 1 Corinthians 10:29-30 "... for why should my freedom be judged by another's conscience? If I take part in the meal with thankfulness, why am I denounced because of something I thank God for?" and "I DO" thank God for His continuing spiritual enlightenments!

So a quiet peace returns to bless my shattered mind because I find that, whatever the world believes about all of these new and very controversial things, I can now thank God over the fact that I was born homosexual. I very much thank God I was cast out from the traditional churches' favor because without me being rejected by the majority of American churches – I never would have been forced to search for deeper, more loving answers in response to the call of the world to continuously condemn itself by insisting on upholding the False Christian freedom and sinful sanctity of accessing Satan's support anytime anyone wants to try to establish a very legalized form of basic human condemnation! Yes, when it comes to establishing legal discrimination Satan is all too willing to support any of those starched and pious Catholic bullet points!

And then, as if to protect my homosexual self-worth, the Holy Spirit shoots Luke 11:52 high into the air, "Woe to you - who think you are experts in the law, because you have taken away the key to knowledge through your unwillingness to share - ALL WITH ALL – Yes, you "experts" yourselves have not entered and you have hindered the honest attempts of those who follow in your footsteps."

And dear God, with me now backing straight away from those False Christian footsteps, this is where I have to say how much "I DO" appreciate all those many wonderful people I have met in my life who can rise above the call to separate and fragment and they always seem to reach out to everyone they meet with such gentle hands that fully grasp the meaning of true spiritual respect.

To forgive or NOT to forgive —That's the Pope's True Christian Test!

With so many different kinds of Christians now yelling, "This is an eternally un-forgivable sin" or directly opposite, "This needs to be forgiven and the issue finally done away with" and with the Catholic hierarchy now verbally stoning me yet while I've had some really great Catholic lay people treat me with such love and respect, it can many times make me wonder about all of the different kinds of Christians I see preaching their own messages in front of me. Compounding the fact that with so many turbulent storms over "morality" seriously approaching, I'm about to be challenged to again think for myself while my sanity appears to be once more threatened by the deeds and actions of "the damning and damned(?)" Catholic Churches' hierarchy.

And yes, Father I confess… I most often identify myself as being an Evangelical. I was baptized in water and I've received the Holy Spirit. I speak and can pray "in tongue." I have had the laying on of hands, as the Bible talks of, and I have felt a presence and an energy I could not explain. I have felt the presence of infinite love and I have also, many times, been in the presence of earthly judgment.

While I am not a practicing Catholic now, I confess, I once lived with a family whose head of the household asked that we, who lived in the house, take training in the ways of Catholics. I have been exposed to the ideology and customs of being Catholic and I respect very much the many wonderful things the Catholic Church has accomplished and created over the years. Mostly, I respect the serious devotion the average everyday Catholics have for their religion, their Church, their Pope and Saints. I CAN see some of the good they do…

But right now, I'm just very confused about some of their core teachings. I'm especially confused about Catholic teachings on the ideology of Jesus' basic forgiveness. With me being from a semi-Catholic background I've said the Lord's Prayer too many times to be confused over the meaning of the core words, "Forgive us as we forgive those who…"

And so with me understanding the soul importance of extending forgiveness, I'm very confused by the Pope's blatant UN-forgiveness! And no, it's not just his un-forgiveness of homosexuals, but more powerfully – I'm locked in a fight with myself over Pope Benedict's un-forgiveness of Judas Iscariot! Yes, I am totally lost and confused over the position Pope Benedict has taken with the new understandings of redemption found within the revelation of the Gospel of Judas. So I wonder am I the crazy Christian or is the Pope the crazy one for not believing what he has now heard?

This is an article from "The Independent" called, The History of Christianity: The Gospel according to Judas. It reads,

Yesterday, a 62-page codex, written from the point of view of the man who betrayed Christ and said to date from the 3rd or 4th century was unveiled in Washington. A seismic moment for the Christian church? Paul Vallely and Andrew Buncombe report.

"It will shake Christianity to its foundations." Or so the pre-publicity suggested. A 3rd or 4th century document called "The Gospel of Judas" was launched upon an unsuspecting world yesterday by no less a biblical authority than the National Geographic magazine, in Washington. Its contents were "explosive" according to Mario Roberty, president of the Swiss foundation which now owns the ancient papyrus manuscript."

Half of the 62-page codex, written in Coptic script, is devoted to an account of the final days of Jesus Christ written from the viewpoint of the man who has for two millennia been excoriated as Christ's deadly betrayer. The text begins: "The secret account of the revelation that Jesus spoke in conversation with Judas Iscariot three days before he celebrated Passover…

And thought the manuscript has been carbon-dated to around 300 A.D. it is likely to be a copy of an earlier Greek manuscript written around the year 150 A.D. in the same period when the gospels of Mark, Matthew, Luke, and John were also written down. So, the new discovery is serious competition, the National Geographic people implied, for the official version.

What The Gospel of Judas says is that, far from being Jesus' enemy, Judas was his chief apostle – who "betrayed" him to the authorities at the actual request of his master in order to fulfill a divine ordinance for the salvation of the world. Judas, alone of the disciples, understood the true significance of Jesus' teachings – because Jesus told him, "You will exceed all of them," Jesus tells the main man in the key passage in the text, "for you will sacrifice the man that clothed me."

Thus the individual whose name has entered the language as a synonym for traitor - selling his master for 30 pieces of silver, the amount for which the Law of Moses specified an Israelite could buy or sell a slave - was, instead of being the big villain, the secret hero.

"The Pharisees... went to Judas and told him.... Although you are evil in this place, you are Jesus' true disciple. And he answered them as they wanted him to. And Judas received the money. And he surrendered him. This is the end of the Gospel of Judas."

Without Judas' help, Jesus would not have been crucified and God's plan to redeem mankind, the Gospel suggests, would not have been fulfilled."

And as I personally fall deeper into the trenches of knowledge of Judas with this new set of information being so truly "explosive" and as I duck and cover from all of the religious fallout I find another enlightening set of thoughts that "in the privacy of my own home" drastically shake my own past views of Christianity to what I once thought of as a rock solid foundation..."

This is by U.S.A. Today, it's entitled,

"Long-lost gospel of Judas casts "traitor" in new light." This is by Dan Vergano and Cathy Lynn Grossman.

Lost for centuries and bound for controversy, the so-called gospel of Judas was unveiled by scholars Thursday. In the article, "The Judas papyrus is one of dozens of gospels found in recent decades whose text fall outside the canon of today's New Testament Bibles. The canon was largely set at the Synod of Rome in 382 when the dominant Christian leaders of the time established the authority of the gospels of Matthew, Mark, Luke, and John as the accepted version of Jesus' birth, life, crucifixion, and resurrection.

Scripture, like history, was codified by the winners, by those who emerged with the greatest numbers at the end of three centuries of Christianity, said Michael White, director of the Institute for the Study of Antiquity and Christian Origins at the University of Texas – Austin. He has counted more than three dozen gospels that didn't make the canonical cut. The ones that did, he said, were not in total harmony but shared a theological view of the passion, the crucifixion and their significance that became the core of the new religion.

"In the ancient world, Christianity was even more diverse than was today." Ehrman said, Not until later centuries did the standard devotional texts known as the New Testament become the bedrock of the Christian faith. Dozens of alternative gospels and creeds lost out in the process."

"The publication team appears to have done everything possible to authenticate the gospel as an ancient work." Said religious scholar Mark Chancey of Southern Methodist University in Dallas, "There seems to be little doubt that it is, indeed, a late third- or early fourth-century work, and not a modern forgery."

Princeton University religious scholar Elaine Pagels, a restoration adviser best known for her work on the Nag Hammadi texts, said, "The gospel of Judas is an astonishing discovery that along with similar texts have in recent years have transformed our understanding of early Christianity."

Experts do see some value in a Bible news flash that prompts modern believers to reexamine the character of Judas....

Other theologians, biblical scholars and pastors say this contrary text is not truly "good news" (the meaning of "gospel") and will make no difference as Easter approaches. The Bible, they say, is a closed book, nearly universally accepted as the official church teachings since the fourth century."

And as I wonder what's more important – "official church teachings" or what Jesus wants us to now learn; then, I reflect on the idea that only a closed mind can believe in the power of "a closed book" so I decide I need to read more…. about Stephen Emmel of Germany's University of Munster, one of the restoration team members saying The Gospel "is an intriguing alternative view of the relationship between Jesus and Judas." Emmel said it also has Jesus relating a new creation myth and account of humankind's origins to Judas, which suggests God didn't create the world, contrary to conventional Christian belief."

Marvin Meyer noted that Judas has often been used by Christians to attack Jews throughout history. "The view of Judas as this evil Jewish person who turned Jesus in fed the flames of anti-Semitism" he said, "so providing a new view of Judas may help counteract such views."

Well to me, what shocked me about all of this legitimate information wasn't the controversial nature of the new biblical find or in my finally comprehending the past real-life history behind book-binding the Bible; but, what really knocked my feet out from under me was Pope Benedict's reaction to the news about Judas Iscariot doing the will of Jesus. Still pointing fingers at others to blame… Pope Benedict refused to officially issue a Catholic blessing or simple pardon.

May God forgive me, but as I think of the Catholic Churches' past (and current?) sexual abuse scandals I wonder how WILL the Catholic Church ever be forgiven for its sins when the Pope and his church hierarchy refuse to officially forgive other people of their trespasses? And I'm blown away by the Pope's basic and raw UN-forgiveness and I think of Pope Benedict's power as a teacher combined with the fact that good teachers always need to be aware of new developments and new information. Yes, good teachers need to be aware of constantly continuing their own personal education. The un-questionable fact is: the best teacher IS a great student! So battling back and forth in my mind I wonder, isn't what unites us all as humans the notion that as teachers the greatest gift we can give our students is to allow the humanity and natural ability of all of us to make a mistake? Plus, what a very high calling to teach our students that at times, yes, even we - as teachers, can make a mistake. The challenge is can we all learn how to make a mistake with grace? But how do we admit it when we've thought the wrong way for so unquestioningly long? The Holy Spirit tells me… just admit I was mistaken - and I admit I HAVE been mistaken over so many of my past Christian concepts, and now with me admitting it… receiving grace is as easy as saying "I'm now ready to extend that forgiveness!" So one day, in our own way at our own pace, we will all question, am I really ready... to be saved by being corrected with grace and by grace - not with just one mistake but with ALL MISTAKES – not with just my own mistakes but in tandem with FORGIVING EVERYONE ELSE'S? And as I do battle with all of these very powerful thoughts I think about the fact that we have all sinned and we all make mistakes and it's all just a matter of time till we all learn to perfectly extend God's Grace. And then I think of Satan and how he can stop us from learning new things, dead in our tracts, just by using our very own stuck-up pride!

So I can't help and pray for a goal... can all the religious teachers of the world show their students how to make a mistake with grace that extends not just within their own self and church family identity but can they now extend grace toward all others as they also make their own very humbling human mistakes – yes, even unto their own personally perceived "biblical enemies"? Yet, now on Earth, it's NOT like heaven because I can still see Satan stirring up all this horse shit going on all around me over people practicing their own brand of SELECT-FORGIVINESS and so I have to contemplate so much more. But as I study quietly on my own and now with a glimmer and a gleam I start to have hope and with the Holy Spirit's help I find a lot more faith in good by simply understanding what bad things happen when we only forgive those we selectively choose too.

Therefore, as I finish reading all of this new information about Judas Iscariot I wonder, so what is God's plan for redeeming mankind? Could God's plan of salvation be just at the center of the strict adherence to only forgiveness – no exceptions? Was Jesus being the most like his Father when he always refused to judge and pronounced, "Father forgive them (all)"?

Therefore I confess, I do wonder how the Pope can, in good conscience, refuse to forgive not just homosexuals or Judas but - ANYONE? I wonder this because the first time I heard of the Gospel of Judas I took it as truly "good news." Yes, I probably ask in vain but why can't the Pope see its healing good news for all of mankind?

And then to hear that Pope Benedict cursed the Gospel of Judas and the damning fact is: Pope Benedict did it right before presiding over his very first Easter Mass.

And I wonder how can Pope Benedict, as a teacher, not welcome the new knowledge of the Gospel of Judas and the forgiveness that it will bring to help heal our shattered UN-forgiving world? Pope Benedict, will Jesus have to say to you personally, "For shame"? How can any of us NOT welcome the good news that anyone and everyone can be forgiven – yes, not just the Catholic Church but even Judas? Because to offer some serious motivation, I do know some people in this world already think of the Catholic Church as being its own kind of traitorous child-abusing False Christian Judas!

So to refute that image, Pope Benedict think how proud Jesus would have been if for your first official Easter Mass you would have emulated words ONLY like Jesus, "Yes, Father, forgive them – this time including – Judas!"

What if Jesus would have wanted to hear a new Pope's first Easter Mass more like this one....

"My fellow Sisters and Brothers in Christ, it is now time to celebrate not the death of Christ but the Resurrection! Thanks to God's grace-filled-plan we have the opportunity to show new life in ourselves by embracing new ways to think and understand by consciously absorbing new and proven authentic information. This is so that we, being united under God's protection and mercy, can bring glory and honor to His Holy Name by injecting into our holy image of one another His Grace.

I, your Pope, would like to make a celebration of my very first Easter Mass with the world by asking the whole world to join with me in a new way to forgive. And it all starts by forgiving our very worst enemy. And I ask that we all - as one - now and forevermore, in the light of new biblical evidence, please forgive Judas Iscariot so that Jesus' chain of atonement may be finally completed by coming full circle back with forgiveness extending from us - as it endlessly extends full circle to also come back to rest on us! Please, everyone, forgive one another each others' pet sins.

Therefore acting as your spiritual teacher and leader of the Catholic Church I ask the world to also join with me in making sure that we all follow the example set by Jesus. Forgive any Judas in your life. And, I ask that each and every one of you, my children, look about you and search your heart, search your mind and see if there is anyone in your life who needs your forgiveness, do not forsake them -because Jesus WILL NOT forsake them! Let us all now forgive one another in love and respect for the love Jesus shows us all. All this we do even as we crucify, not each other, but we crucify the demons we find within our own selfish selves that so many times stop us from forgiving, stop us from loving, Satan stops us from sharing God's Immensely Powerful Grace!

And now that we have all forgiven each and every Judas that we know – let us be thankful our Father who art in heaven has now forgiven us just as much! Let us worship now and forever more the resurrection of the soul that total forgiveness and enlightenment brings to us all - to each and every one." Amen.

But then like a bolt from the blue, I am zapped from my fantasy of the "Perfect Pope" who teaches only peace and UN-conditional love - as things now start to get, in a very real worldly way, two-fisted pointedly ugly.

Vatican criticizes "fantasy"

This is an article by Stacy Meichtry with Religion Service.

Vatican City – A Vatican official, preaching in front of Pope Benedict XVI at a recent Mass, denounced "The Da Vinci Code" novel and a highly publicized Gospel of Judas as examples of profit-driven propaganda aimed at exploiting Christianity... The Rev. Raniero Cantalamessa, the official, "preacher of the papal household," criticized the texts during a April 14th Mass at St. Peter's Basilica, commemorating the death of Christ on the cross.

"These are things that do not merit attention in this time and place, but we cannot allow the silence of the faithful to be misunderstood as embarrassment and let the good faith of millions of people get grossly manipulated by the media," Cantalamessa said. The criticism came one day after Benedict called Judas a "double-crossing liar," reaffirming the traditional portrayal of Judas as a traitor who identified Jesus to Jewish authorities in exchange for blood money, sparking events that led to the crucifixion. "He was greedy. Money was more important to him than communion with Jesus, more important than God and His love." Benedict said.

And as I read Pope Benedict's words calling Judas a "double-crossing liar' and Benedict saying, "He was greedy. Money was more important to him...."

I think of where in the Holy Bible it is written: John 18:4-9

Jesus, knowing all that was going to happen to him, went out and asked them, "Who is it you want?" "Jesus of Nazareth," they replied. "I am he." Jesus said. (And Judas the traitor was standing there with them.) When Jesus said, "I am he" they drew back and fell to the ground. Again he asked them, "Who is it that you want?" And they said, "Jesus of Nazareth" "I told you that I am he," Jesus answered, "If you are looking for me then let these men go." This happened so that the words he had spoken would be fulfilled. "I have not lost one of those you gave me."

So logically to me, if Jesus purposefully went out to meet the soldiers who came to take him away, and the soldiers bowed down to Jesus and didn't really want to take him away ... so how can any of us not say that Jesus went with the soldiers willingly or deliberately? Isn't that a sign Jesus was NOT fighting back OR afraid and instead Jesus was cooperating all the way? Why is it so hard to think that Judas also was "standing by Jesus" yes, Judas was totally co-operating fully just as Jesus had told him so...

Then with John 10:17-18 Jesus said, "The reason my Father loves me is that I lay down my life only to take it up again. No one takes it from me, but I lay it down of my own accord. I have authority to lay it down and authority to take it up again. This command I received from my Father."

So to the Holy See, I confess that convinces me beyond the shadow of a spiritual-deathly-doubt....Jesus said, "No one takes it from me, but I lay it down of my own accord" and between the fact that A Course in Miracles teaches that Judas is well loved by Jesus, and with the Gospel of Judas saying also Judas was doing Jesus' will, compounding that with the Bible teaching me that even if worst case scenario Judas was a bad guy I'm still supposed to forgive him so that my sins are forgiven, it's then I come to a "heretical" decision. I'm taking a contrary to Catholic teaching stand and I believe Judas is with Jesus right now, at his right hand, and definitely beloved by Jesus. So no, no-one can ever get me to believe that Jesus was-ever or could-ever be betrayed especially with

Jesus' ability to always read other people's thoughts! So no, I'm sorry, not even a "Holy Pope" can now convince me to buy into the concept Jesus was, in the past, ever betrayed. And then I thank God for all of the times I've read the Bible when all alone, strictly by myself!

Then logically, as I contemplate more on receiving all of my own God-sent mental therapy, maybe the real gospel truth is the only one we can - really betray - is our own self - when first we project our own feelings onto others?

So right now with all of this unholy warring still raging on, I'm just feeling strangely confused about how I really should feel about the Pope's inerrancy, the Catholic Church's hierarchy, and their combined official teachings that promote the UN-forgiveness, as a chain reaction, of only - other peoples' sin?

But, to think in a more positive light instead of just thinking about doctrines and hard-nosed hard-liners, I'll think of the wonderful friends I've met that are Catholics and I thank God for all the times that they've been there for me. I thank God for the times my Catholic friends generously prayed for me. And with my road ahead now getting even bumpier and filled with so many different sets of cracks and deep ruts - I know I'll always need as many love-filled prayers as I can get!

Therefore to help calm this confusion I'm experiencing while I'm trapped in this Christian combative zone, I now focus on the positive words of Jesus, "I have not lost one of those you gave me." "I have not lost one of those you gave me" like a mantra of love, I repeat Jesus' words – "I have not lost one of those you gave me."

So, as I finish reflecting on holy wars, traitors, being betrayed and to dealing with the real "double-crossing liar"... I now wonder if Satan is laughing at us every time we think we find someone unworthy enough for any of us to NOT-forgive? Do you think Satan smiles every time we fight and bicker over our rituals, traditions, or who has the – right or wrong quotes? Will Satan just sinfully strive to get us to condemn one another for all of time? I just know I worship Jesus and I thank Him that His love is so strong and so powerful that not even Judas Iscariot or Pope Benedict or I, as a homosexual, will ever be lost from Jesus' watchful eyes and protective arms! And dear God, please bless Jesus for Him never ever turning His back to any of us that have ever felt like lonely and abandoned sacrificial lambs....

But as I'm sinfully reminded of those who DO turn their backs to their fellow brothers and sisters, from the dark side of my mind I hear Satan laughing as he tries to tempt me to once again believe in the justification of SEVERLY punishing those who break "Biblical Law!" And, yes, especially punish those who profess to - teach - the law! It's then I hear Satan quote the Bible while he reads James 3:1 "Not many of you should presume to be teachers, my brothers, because you know that we who teach will be judged more strictly" And as I flinch while I now hear Satan howling.... I think of his devilishly double perception humor....... And of course remembering 2 Corinthians 11:13 with the ability of the Angel of Darkness to "quote and deceive" what's found in the light just to get us to continue to hate each other for ANY reason.... I realize with my own many inner weaknesses I still have a long way to personally go before I can reach that pinnacle of always extending to everyone perfect love.

So I thank God that Our Father who art in heaven has the power to save us all – even when that means He has to save us from our own Mistaken Human Teachings. Ironically, in a very queer twist of fate, I wonder if for all of the "teacher's mistakes" the Pope has possibly made in his life will his True punishment, if he continues to promote the ideology of punishment, be that when he finally does get to heaven he will have to give up all of his worldly artwork and treasures to forever concentrate on only the words found in John 13:12-17?

Besides I have God's hope, maybe at some point before the pontiff meets Jesus face to face he will reconsider and be willing to stand up humbly, as one of the world's major teachers, and officially repent of past views - and grabbing the "traditional helm" change the direction of his now very Catholic Titanic as it goes full steam ahead... totally ramming itself blind-sighted into the core of some of its own self-condemning UN-forgiving ideologies!

I can only pray that with a deep inner-awakening of love maybe the Pope will one day be open to the idea that if by some strange twist of God's fate Judas WAS Jesus' most enlightened disciple, well, I know I sure wouldn't want my name to be written down in the Book of Life as being the Holy See to publically call Jesus' most advanced disciple... "a money grubbing, double-crossing, greedy liar" - especially when it's public knowledge that the Pope's very own house of worship isn't in that perfect of an order! And suddenly I wonder, what would the Pope say, for an excuse, if Jesus told him directly to his face, "Yes, you were PROJECTING when you, as the Pope, said, "Money was more important to him than communion with God! And as far as I'm concerned, you're very much a true Benedict – a Benedict Arnold"

And, dear God, with me realizing those last very private inner-thoughts – I confess, I'm very, very frightened because….. I'm not really sure if that last thought came from Satan or if thinking of the Pope projecting his own failings onto Judas is an affirmation sent straight from the Holy Spirit!

So, after all of this crazy Catholic combat, what have I learned? Yes dear Lord, on earth as it is in heaven – sometimes some things are best played by playing it totally forgivingly safe! So maybe it's best for me to NOT give into Satan's temptation… that causes me to lose SO much respect for the Pope's teacher-reputation.

And, with the thought of totally fighting Satan in my own mind, perhaps it's time for me to go into my own personal prayer closet, shut that black drape and now, from the depths of my ever loving soul, I'll try to genuinely forgive the Pope's Royal Catholic Church for very publically committing some very seriously blatantly hypocritical biblical sins and yet, for my own peace of mind, I will also try to put the knowledge of their very abusive sex scandals forever out of my mind. But the next time I hear the Pope preach against Saint Judas or same-sex marriage or of the "evils" of homosexuality, well, I'll just be forced to pray to be released from my own deep despair at seeing a human teacher who may be way too proud and embarrassed to admit ALL of his own very UN-loving, Un-gracious, Un-bending mistakes.

But I do wonder that if the Catholic Church IS right in that sins have levels and degrees and some are worse than others… with some sins being totally "un-forgivable" ….it is then my own words come back to haunt me as I wonder – "which is worse" – the sin committed by people who sin with each other consentingly or the sin committed un-consentingly to a child? So again I'm torn in two and divided as I wonder can any sin no matter what sin be forgiven completely 100% or not at all?

It then makes me glad I'm not the one who has to judge and decide the worldly legalities… My job, it seems, right now is just to be open to question all of my own deeply held past beliefs and to seek for ANY remaining sanity and the Holy Spirit's authentic good gospel of True Christian Love!

Currently, for me to try to reposition, hunting to gain a clearer perspective, knowing everyone is vulnerable in battle — it's time I pray for my own damn self.... And as I, on bended knee, mark the sign of the Trinity — touching my head, heart and both shoulders, I very much pray for the Holy Spirit to be able to expand and increase my own self-awareness of when I very humanly sometimes do "not" forgive. So I again repent, strictly I promise to forgive NOT just me, myself, and I.... but I DO PROMISE TO FORGIVE the Pope for hurting me, as a homosexual, and I forgive him with the same equal amount of forgiveness that I personally would like to receive from him in return.... Then, as I meditate on the power of forgiveness, quite unexpectedly with the sound of a mighty crack of the whip, the storm clouds lashing overhead temporarily part while a ray of pure sunshine radiates down as I hear words I NEVER, ever thought I would hear.

I now hear the words that His Holiness Pope Benedict XVI has formally renounced his past opposition to the use of condoms and will promote their use as a means to prevent and untold amount of "worldly" suffering and pain and confronted with "the lesser of two evils" I confess, it's the Pope's "new message" that is a truly blessed message that gives me life-saving critical hope that..... "God CAN surprise us" One and ALL! So I thank my Holy Father in Heaven that the Holy Father on Earth is in the slow, sleepy blinking of an eye, "TRANSFIGURING AND TRANSFORMING" quite possibly - EVOLVING — right in front of my gay and now happy soul and as I smile I realize maybe God CAN teach an old dog new tricks. And God KNOWS, at times, I can definitely relate to being just an old, lonely lost dog seeking shelter from a violent, destructive storm!

My Old and Crumbling Ideologies

I was first introduced to "A Course in Miracles" back in the early 1980's. Not only does God work in mysterious ways but He has always seemed to have taught me the most powerful of lessons while catching me off-guard and totally by surprise, yes I finally surrendered to Him, and now I know why it's best not to judge Him, or limit Him. My God is not only a loving God but He is a God of many unexpected gifts, given at unexpected times for no expected reason!

This crucial gift He gave to me called A Course in Miracles is not just a regular book. It turns out A Course in Miracles is a totally Jesus inspired Holy Book, its one book among many that all teach different people about the same God while using different histories, and languages and mental understandings.

For me even being introduced to the book teaching me how to better myself at receiving miracles was itself the first of many unexplainable miracles to come. But to me, receiving this enlightening book was also a very important mile-stone on my inner journey of learning to trust love and find understanding in life.

Once upon a time, a long time ago, I truly believed that there was only "One-Way" to get and keep God's grace and mercy. I was required by Evangelical Law to share the gospel and save as many other souls as I could – conversion is taught as a moral duty - priority number one. Well, one day my own life turned very much upside down as I tried "to save" a dear friend of mine.

It was then God gave me one of the most important teaching books of my life. While I was talking to my friend Paula about her reading the

Bible more, she made a turn-around deal with me! Paula said that she would read the Bible more if I would be willing to read "A Course in Miracles." Because we were friends that respected each other we met in the middle, shook hands, and we both walked away with very complex books to study.

It wasn't until much later in my life did I realize what an about face that was to be in my life. "The Course" (as it is affectionately called) has enlightened me to the point that my mind has been at war with itself for many, many, years!

Just as the Bible says there are two kinds of Christians, it now seems there are also two ways of looking at the crucifixion of Jesus. Take for example, "The message of the Crucifixion" found in the book called - A Course in Miracles. See what you may be open to understand as Jesus steps up in front of the world and saying with a clear strong voice:

"If the Apostles had not felt guilty, they never could have quoted me as saying, "I come not to bring peace but a sword" This is clearly the opposite of everything I taught. Nor could they have described my reactions to Judas as they did, if they had really understood me. I could not have said, "Betrayest thou the Son of Man with a kiss?" unless I believed in betrayal. The whole message of the crucifixion was simply that I did not. The "punishment" I was said to have called forth upon Judas was a similar mistake. Judas was my brother and a Son of God, as much a part of the Sonship as myself. Was it likely that I would condemn him when I was ready to demonstrate that condemnation is impossible? As you read the teachings of the Apostles, remember that I told them myself that there was much they would understand later, because they were not wholly ready to follow me at the time. I do not want you to allow any fear to enter into the thought system toward which I am guiding you. I do not call for martyrs but for teachers. No one is punished for sin, and the Sons of God are not sinners."

It was about at this point during my first time reading this passage that my evangelical fundamentalist Christian foundations began to soften, crumble and collapse, like an old abandoned house of mud built on sand. My mind flashes thoughts of all of the traditional teachings of my very traditional Christian past. So many assumptions, so many lines that were drawn in the sand, my most fundamental concepts of the Christianity I was taught are now literally just falling apart! While "shock and awe" sets in during which I have a hard time processing the statements – I do NOT call for martyrs - and - the Sons of God are NOT sinners! So my mind races to the hilt to question and understand more.

But as my original fundamentalist teachings still come to mind I wonder if what I just read in "the Course" of miracles IS true then with Biblical opposites and contrasts like these there may yet be hell to pay for Satan and those False Christian prophets who have planted bad seeds and wrong quotations in the field called the Holy Bible. Now I have to wonder if the False Christians have taken our Christ's message of free Grace and redemption and by their ignorance or in their False-Pride, have they marched God's grace down to the auctioneer's square where so many of God's free-gifts are now bought and then re-sold and it's all done, all paid for, with just those basic core beliefs of past-lies dedicated to the god called "truly easy" financial Mammon?

Misquoted? Misquoted? – Misquoted!!!

So with my strict fundamentalist ideologies crumbling all around me, I have to ask myself, was Jesus Christ really misquoted in the Bible? And if so, was Jesus misquoted by accident or on purpose? What can I do other than open myself up to learn, open myself up and now truly question? And I do know I have, since a child, ALWAYS questioned the idea of Jesus swinging a sword. Especially when I understand by Jesus' actions that He came only to serve and to save, Jesus only acted in peace! So, is the concept of Jesus saying he came to bring a sword the biggest and most destructive of the False Christian lies? I just know seeing Jesus with a sword in his hand just doesn't make ANY DAMN SENSE - period! Especially when I contrast the biblical words of Jesus saying, "I come NOT to bring peace but a sword" with its direct biblical opposite found in Matthew 26:52-54… Put your sword back in its place Jesus said to him. "For all who draw the sword will die by the sword. Do you think I cannot call on my Father and he will at once put at my disposal more than 12 legions of angels… but how then would the Scriptures be fulfilled that say it must happen in this way?"

But, here I am in the midst of this Holy War against Homosexuals trying to get a grip of all this contrary and confusing new information that's tearing my mind and heart apart. Information like Judas was a good guy after all? Now, with A Course in Miracles, I am told also not only was Judas a good and well-loved disciple but more importantly – NO ONE is punished for sins and that as I repeat it to myself, "The Sons of God are NOT sinners!" I just go WOW!

Talk about a conflict of understanding! The basic tenet of the Southern Baptist – Assembly of God – kind of Christianity I was raised to believe is that - first and foremost – as Sally Kern reiterated - we are all born sinners who need to repent, accept Jesus, and of course, we WILL be punished for our sins! All of the traditional churches I have gone to have all taught punishment and hell awaited those who disobey the Ten Commandments. It was stressed to me that we are all born into a world of evil and sin and that we can only be redeemed through the blood and sacrifice of Jesus Christ. We must all be "washed in the blood" and this is because according to the Bible, "All have fallen short of the glory of God."

I was taught by the churches of my youth that in God's eyes all humans are miserable sinners with the devil's hand upon our hearts until we first see the light, confess our sins and repent, and accept salvation by honoring God, Jesus, and the laws of many commandments. And "naturally," we must also strive to honor the rites and rituals of our very own private and individual preacher and church of choice.

But now with all of these many varied thoughts, questions, and quotes firing directly at me it seems to me I can always choose to dodge the main issues and stay blind and never ever question what the majority of the churches in the world now believe. Or, I can admit to myself - I've come too far, I've been hurt way too deep, I have to journey on to see this Holy War against Homosexuals Parable thru to the very end!

And to those who preach... "Hell is a place you will be sent to after you die," I now say, I know hell to be a current conflict of warring thoughts about who is right about what is to be considered.... so God damned biblically WRONG?

So back and forth in my mind I flip from – Not peace but extreme division!

Luke 12:51 And Jesus said, "Do you think I came to bring peace on earth? No I tell you, but division." And as I wonder if this quote is another false divisive bad seed I think of all of the preachers who have preached on the importance of dividing yourself away from those people who are judged to be evil... yes, you to have to first judge (which is totally the opposite of non-judgment) and then separate yourself away from "those kinds" of bad people...

But because I reason, I fight back that there are clearly two ways to perceive all things. So I debate if the division in Luke12:51 is Jesus dividing people apart, as a conservative evangelical would believe. Or, is the division Jesus is talking about the inner-kind-of-division found in each and every one of us as we all personally battle our own thoughts of choosing to love vs. choosing to discriminate? Because of humanities' premeditated judgment is society involved in just an outer-war of dividing up people against one another while playing the game of "I'm" good vs. "you're" evil? Or is it simply - our world is innocently caught up in societies' individuals' inner-private-wars of guilt, shame, projecting, and pointing at other people to blame? The Bible tells me we all have inner-quarreling going on and so I think of societies members who are always bemoaning and berating so it's now understandable that Satan finds a way to distract us from the fact that our war mentality has just naturally extended from an-inner-to-an-outer reality! And as we concentrate on the outer fighting at the expense of the inner learning, I wonder, in the end, which war will stop first - our outer-wars or do we have to heal our inner-wars first? And then another bullet of division shoots by me as the Holy Spirit reminds me of John 9:16 "Some of the Pharisees said, "This man is not from God, for he does not keep the Sabbath." But others asked, "How can a sinner do such miraculous signs? – So they were divided!"

And realizing that Jesus did cause people to be individually-divided over his miracles and whether or not he was the Son of God.... once again I'm reminded that the choices made of: we are sinners or saints... God wants martyrs or gentle teachers.... and, of course, those words are very holy or totally unholy.... Yes, those choices of meaning are always a state of mind and are guided by our own inner-voices!

And then I thank God for the Holy Spirit and the Holy Bible because when 1 John 2:27 comes into my mind I feel the love of the Holy Spirit envelope me, "As for you, the anointing you received from him remains in you, and – you to not need ANYONE to teach you."

And then my inner-voice teaches me in John 16:12 Jesus said, "I have much more to say to you, more than you can now bear. But when he, the Spirit of truth comes, he will guide you into all truth. He will not speak on his own, he will speak only what he hears, and he will tell you what is yet to come." And as I think of what is yet to come in the future and how God IS still teaching His Children at the pace and rate we are willing to hear what He has to say, I now wonder.... John 12:25 "Jesus did many other things as well. If every one of them were written down I suppose that even the whole world would not have room for the books that would be written."

And then I find myself coming to terms and to peace with the fact that just like the New Testament upgraded the Old Testament, now maybe A Course in Miracles has come down from the heavens to try and evolve us and take us above and beyond just constantly – Fighting over our traditions and the way we worship our many ways of stinking-old-thinking!

Finally the Holy Spirit within me says, "And to give praise back to Jesus, He gave Me the best of introductions" as John 14:26-27 settles into my mind.... I'm reminded of Jesus' kind words of the Comforter again, "But the Counselor, the Holy Spirit, whom the Father will send in my name will teach you all things and will remind you of everything I have said to you. Peace I leave with you, my peace I give to you. I do not give to you as the world gives do not let your hearts be troubled and DO NOT BE AFRAID!"

So now I can thank God that I don't have to be afraid of new concepts and new thoughts and finally 2,000 years after Jesus' resurrection, I can tell that even though I'm sometimes still afraid of my fellow Christian brothers and sisters, humanity IS starting to be mentally re-awakened by being ready to comprehend the highly evolved and very intricate conceptions found within A Course in Miracles. And yet again, I thank my Father in heaven that in 1982 I was personally ready to be "traditionally" de-programmed and mentally graduate to a higher level of consciousness thanks to my friend Paula's gift of Christ-like-charity. Then I think, how ironic, that while I was trying to "save Paula's soul" – Paula Martin saved MY SOUL by giving me a book that would eventually play a major-roll in saving my.... True Christian SANITY!

And thanks to A Course in Miracles I have realized once and for all the important "core-value" that, as a homosexual, I DON'T have to choose between my love for God and who I am! I finally know God

DOES love me unconditionally even when - some Christians - "choose to" - deny - that very blessed fact!

I only pray that what I have learned will one day extend, gently on the wings of a dove, to fly all around the world to land in the hands of all gay children's parents. This so that they may finally realize - they also - no longer have to make that unholy choice of being forced to decide to love making "a god" out of their Church; OR instead, in True Christ-like Freedom they can now love seeing…. their Own CHILD'S Happiness – completely fulfilled!

So as I embrace the idea of all straight parents embracing all of their own homosexual children it gives me great hope and out of my hope I now pray for all False Christians the "False Christian's Prayer" found in Matthew 13:14-15

"You will be ever hearing but never understanding; you will be ever seeing but never perceiving. For this people's heart has become calloused; they hardly hear with their ears AND THEY HAVE CLOSED THEIR EYES. Otherwise they might see with their eyes hear with their ears, UNDERSTAND WITH THEIR HEARTS and turn, and I would heal them."

Yes, dear Loving God, I pray, "Please heal them of their False Christian's calloused heart's DESIRE TO…STILL PROMOTE - anyone else's - CRUCIFIXION!"

And dear God, please give us ALL the wisdom to know when we should personally close our own mouths to prevent influencing the cold, closing off of…. someone else's heart!

A Legal War of Words

O ur legal battle field can get to be a hell-of-a smoke and mirrors maze to navigate when we're left dealing with only dissention and people who will not see anyone else's point of view other than their own. So maybe to try and make some semblance of peace, it's time for us to figure out the boundaries and lines that we Americans draw between human rights, Federal rights, and the rights of individual children OR adults to create their own inner and outer reality while they still maintain their ability to allow other people the fundamental rights necessary to create also - their own. Where is the all elusive middle ground that society needs to keep itself from self-destructing when courting extremely polarizing points of view? If individuals can commit suicide that means society, as a whole, is also capable of mass-suicide and self-destruction. With all of the wars on this... and war over that... I wonder if Satan's all ready getting us to self-destruct and we're just blindly doing it to an un-aware degree? When I think of how much time, energy, and money is burned up producing a living nightmare for so many basically innocent people while society's children and elderly and disabled are neglected, forgotten or continuously abused - it makes me wonder where do we, as humanity, go from here? To hell, I hope NOT!

So, out of necessity, back onto the battle field of immoral religious wars fought over different ideologies about private worship while we draw lines between people, states, country, and common rights; and yes, there is a very fine line between keeping one's own personality and identity and by someone crossing a line – one person ends up being submissively subservient to another person's identity and very human ego.

Just like children that are disciplined and sometimes worldly punished in an effort to get the children to listen to the wishes of the parent, where do we draw the boundary with how much control of the child's INTELLECT – the Parent has – like the State has, like the Federal government has – to tell an individual child what to do when inter-reacting with the rest of common society? More pressing, when do we need to protect a child from its own parents past biases to help that child grow up to be – FREE FROM ANY DISTRUCTIVE, disruptive, UNHEALTHY BIASES?

But, until the day comes that we can remove all negative prejudices from everyone on earth, what a challenge for society to keep its individual members from destroying one another. Like an auto-immune disease is to the human body is the battle over equality the toughest one to win because we're only fighting our own self-destructive selves? How many wars are now being fought over just basic human rights and dignity? Too many I think and what may turn out to be our biggest war yet will be the war over how States and the Federal government define the line between a child's intellect - and its very own family - and when the government needs to intercede to prevent mental or physical injury to any or all? These are some hard and very difficult issues for us all to grapple with. But the most important legal question of all is: How will society and its governing bodies give all of its individual members balance and harmony with one another while still permitting us all the greatest amount of individual God-given freedom – with the ultimate in equal safety and equal justice for all? In America only the Supreme Court will say.

And if I ever got a chance at inter-reacting with the Supreme Court Justices these are some tough questions I would respectfully ask... So which is considered to be of more importance in America - Human Rights and Dignity - or - Federal/State Law, especially when Federal or State laws hinder or impede any humans' core rights? Which value is the most valuable emotionally – family rights poised under the banner of "family values" or - is an individual's personal right to live in peace and harmony with all of society and its many diverse and very different religions, laws, and ideas of what even the word freedom means – is this the most important for all of us to value? I ask these difficult questions because what happens to us as a nation when to get along in society I, as an individual, need information to help me understand- myself - or the world I live in but my parents value keeping me in the dark and uneducated on an issue that they as individual people find offensive? The prime example is when a parent doesn't want their child to be mentally exposed to the knowledge that there are different religions or sexual orientations to be acknowledged, i.e. when Sally Kern, acting as a State Rep., tried to create a law in Oklahoma that bans children from having access to children's books that are designed specifically - to teach children - how to get along with, and be aware of, people in society with different kinds of religious, romantic, sexual, or familial orientations? I personally don't see how any society can internally survive for the duration without its individual members positively learning to cooperate with at least a basic level of common decency and understanding.

And yet, what also becomes of an individual person who is born into a family in which that family's personal core-value is centered-around valuing bigotry or hate or exclusion of anyone else who claims the freedom of a different self-expression? I ask because with all of the wars over family and religious values going on right now we are at a cross-road in destiny where we have to decide, as a whole-society – how much power does any family have to over-power their own individual child's need and right to an honest education that will teach that child, first and foremost, how to get along with the rest of society without that child growing up with an inner-core-desire to over-come another individual member of society? Will teaching society's children to all get along be the best defense for us to use on both over-powering the "War on Terror" and nullifying an individual's base human need to take a personal offense over a base human prejudice? Aren't bullies - and their wars - just the physical manifestation of what happens when a child eventually grows up to despise other religions, races, or ideologies that lead to different mental and/or physical/sexual expressions? For society to keep itself from self-destructing we need to teach ALL children to understand and even try to respect those people whose views are different! Please be aware I said, "Respect those people" not necessarily "respect those views." But to - respect those people - is it a matter of just teaching all people that a bad view doesn't necessarily make a person inherently BAD or EVIL? And, while separating – a view- from – a person - if, by chance, any person does want to cling to a bad religious view they still "have the right" to maintain their bad view... so as long as they are willing to "Leave to God the things of God" when it comes down to understanding other people also have, in tandem, the legal right to maintain their own different set of religious views – with NO repercussions or undue harassment. And as far as, "What's natural," we always have the natural freedom to call on the American Psychological Association to separate for us - the "False from the True-REALITY!"

So, speaking of different views AND – battling False-freedom of religion – what I personally want to know is: Do I really have – FREEDOM OF RELIGION - here in America? What if my religious views are to be centered strictly around the view that all people will be saved? Do I really have the freedom, in the good ol' U.S. of A., to believe that God is powerful enough to - eventually - save us all? Or, are Christian beliefs only counted or recognized in America when someone "values" the thought of getting to personally sit in the judgment seat while condemning other people to hell for eternal damnation? I, myself, personally value the thought that GOD LOVES US ALL EQUALLY! And personally, what a difference that very thought makes in how I think of, and treat - ALL PEOPLE! And yes, in my mind, if someone still wants to believe in a hell all I can say is, "Be careful what you wish for – because as we sow, we DO reap, so – I wonder - don't people think what will happen to their own personal soul when anyone will end up getting the very kind of hell anyone's now willing to curse and condemn ANYONE else too?" And naturally, a hate-filled condemning kind of mind is a hell of a waste of mind – whatever your religious point of view may currently be!

So not to make things more complicated than they all ready are but we also need to be aware of what happens when a child eventually grows up to find out that they are internally different from their parents and then the parents become upset because they, as parents, wanted to mold their child into an exact replica of those self-same parents – for sometimes purely egotistical reasons. How does society protect all children, yes, including homosexual children, from the consequences of their own personal family's individual and sometimes self-destructive or manipulative egos? While there are two kinds of Christians there are also two kinds of parents as well, some are positive and some are negative, some teach unconditional love while some teach unending hate, some parents are totally supportive while some are most definitely – NOT.. So, I believe society has an overwhelming need to promote its individual members to gain - the education - that allows all people to be able to work, worship, respect, and relate one to another as fellow human beings - for the benefit of the individual child - for the benefit of the whole world. I believe God would want society, while promoting the greater good, to have the shared-right to make sure every individual child is given the highest and most truthful education. Because children are not born hating, - themselves or others, - it seems that right now "parent's-rights" are promoted over "children's-rights" and because "the sins of the fathers are passed down to their children" and some parents want to teach their children hate, aggression, separation, or superiority – we now live in a world centered around so much unnecessary conflict. So I can only hope that one day society and individual families will join together, as one, in a blending of sharing the right to enlighten and protect all children by all parties involved promoting a full education based on logic, reasoning, and above it all, tolerance and acceptance for all of the other members of society – even with those people who we may personally choose to politely, non-violently disagree with.

I pray to God because He wants us all to get along by us learning to understand and accept other people's religions and faiths. Words do mean different things in different languages to different people and I believe all of the world's religious fighting is based on simply just a war over the meaning we perceive in our and other people's choices of words - for the Bible tells me so....

Ephesians 4:29 "Do not let any unwholesome talk come out of your mouths, but only what is helpful for building others up according to their needs..."

But in our holy war of many different points of extreme views I see... 2 Timothy 2:23-26 "Don't have anything to do with foolish and stupid arguments, because you know they produce quarrels and the Lord's servant must not quarrel, instead he must BE KIND TO EVERYONE, able to teach, not resentful. Those who oppose him he must gently instruct, in the hope that God will grant them repentance leading to a knowledge of the truth and that they will come to their senses – and escape from the trap of the devil who has taken them captive to do his will."

So don't you believe God would tell us all to now escape the traps of Satan's hate by… 1 Peter 3:8-9 "Finally, all of you, live in harmony with one another, be sympathetic, love as brothers, be compassionate and humble. Do not repay evil with evil, or insult with insult, but with blessing, because to this you were called so that you may inherit a blessing"

I just wonder how society would treat itself if instead of some Christians teaching our Muslim, Jewish, and yes, even homosexual brothers and sisters that they are just miserable sinners what if we made James 4:1-3 our conceptual banner instead, "What causes fights and quarrels among you? Don't they come from your desires that battle within you? You want something but don't get it. You kill and covet, but you cannot have what you want. You quarrel and fight. You do not have, because you do not ask God. When you ask, you do not receive because you ask with THE WRONG MOTIVES – that you may spend what you get on your own pleasures." And then 1 Peter 4:8-9 says, "Above all, love each other deeply, because love covers over a multitude of sins. Offer hospitality to one another without grumbling." And then Romans 16:17-18 "I urge you brothers to watch out for those who cause divisions and put obstacles in your way that are contrary to the teachings you have learned keep away from them. For such people are not serving our Lord Christ, but their own appetites. By smooth talk and flattery they deceive the minds of naïve people."

Therefore, when our unified society finally realizes the extent to which some of its members have been deceiving and been deceived just by Satan's-smooth-talk, flattery, and back-scratching – it is then that this next news article quickly smashes apart all of the naivety and makes totally perfect… logical sense….

"Today's wars are less about ideas than extreme tribalism" This article was written by David Ronfeldt and was published by The Christian Science Monitor. David Ronfeldt is a senior political scientist at the RAND Corporation, a nonprofit research organization, and the author of "Al Qaeda and Its Affiliates: A Global Tribe Waging Segmental Warfare?"

He writes, "Western strategists and policymakers should stop talking about a clash of civilizations and focus on the real problem: extreme tribalism. Recent events – riots in many nations protesting cartoons of the prophet Muhammad, Sunni-Shiite warring in Iraq, the Taliban resurgence in Afghanistan – confirm that the West is not in a clash with Islam. Instead, Islam, which is a civilizing force, has fallen under the sway of Islamists who are a tribalizing force. Unfortunately, the tribalism theme has difficulty gaining traction. After the end of the cold war, many American strategists preferred the optimistic "end of history" idea that democracy would triumph around the world, advanced by France's Jacques Fukuyama in 1989. A contrary notion – reversion to tribalism – made better sense to other strategists, such as France's Jacques Attali in 1992. Indeed, the emergence of ethnic warring in the Balkans and elsewhere confirmed that when societies crumble, people revert to tribal and clan behaviors that repudiate liberal ideals. Perhaps partly because the idea of "tribalism" sounds too anthropological for modern strategists, it has not taken hold. American thinking has shifted to revolve around a more high-minded but less accurate concept: "the clash of civilizations" articulated by Samuel Huntington in 1993.

But what troubles the world is far more a travel of tribalisms than a clash of civilizations. The major clashes are not between civilizations per se, but between antagonistic segments that are fighting across fringe border zones (like Christian Serbs vs. Muslim Kosovars), or feuding within the same civilization, such as Sunnis vs. Shiites in Iraq.

Most antagonists, no matter how high-mindedly they proclaim their ideals, are operating in terribly tribal and clannish ways. Some, such as Al Qaeda terrorists, are extreme tribalists who dream of making the West start over at a razed, tribal level.

This travail is sure to persist, fueling terrorism, ethnonationalism, religious strife, sectarian feuds, and clannish gang violence and crime. Thus, the cartoon protest riots pose an effort to mobilize an Islamic global tribe, not a civilization. Al Qaeda and its affiliates comprise an information age network, but they, too, operate like a global tribe: decentralized, segmental, lacking in central hierarchy, egalitarian toward kith and kin, ruthless towards others.

What are tribes like? The tribe was the first major form of social organization. The hierarchy, market, and network forms developed ages later. Classic tribes are ruled by kinship principles about blood and brotherhood that fix one's sense of identity and belonging. Tribes are also egalitarian and segmental. Everyone is deemed equal and must share. Each part, such as a clan, is structured similarly, aiming for self-sufficiency. And there is no formal chief, though a "big man" may arise. Democracy may appear in tribal councils, but it is not liberal, since it does not tolerate minority rights and dissident views once a consensus emerges.

What maintains order in a tribe is not hierarchy and law — it is too early a form for that — but kinship principles stressing mutual respect, dignity, pride, and honor. Reciprocal gift giving is essential. Humiliating insults upset peace more than anything else, for an insult to one is seen as an insult to everyone of that lineage. And there are only two ways to restore honor: compensation or revenge. Finally, a tribe may view itself as a realm of virtue, but see outsiders as a different realm that may be treated differently, even brutally, especially if they are "different."

Much of the world is still like this. Of particular concern to strategists, a dense arc of tribal and clan systems runs across North Africa, the Middle East, and South Asia, up into the "stans" of Central Asia. Even modern societies still have tribal cores and impulses. That shows in their cultures, nationalisms, identity politics, kindred glues like sports clubs and social fads, and in cronyism, nepotism, and gang life. Tribalism, for good and ill, is alive everywhere, all the time. We just don't think about it much, and use other terms.

So let's shift away from the civilization paradigm. The tribalism paradigm is better for illuminating the crucial problem: the tribalization of religion. The more that extremists create divisions between "us" and "them," vainly claim sacredness solely for their own ends, demonize others, revel in codes of revenge, crave territorial and spiritual conquests, and suppress moderates who disagree — all the while claiming to act on behalf of a deity — the more their religious orientation becomes utterly tribal and prone to wreaking violence of the darkest kind. They can only pretend to represent a civilization.

The "war of ideas" should be rethought. Western leaders keep pressing Muslim leaders everywhere to denounce terrorism as uncivilized. But this approach, plus counter pressures from sectarian Islamists, has put moderate Muslims on the defensive, stymieing them from speaking out. An approach that focuses on questioning extreme tribalism may be more effective at freeing up dialogue and inviting a search for common, ecumenical ground.

Shifting to a travail-of-tribalisms perspective would have to be carefully thought out. The point is not to condemn all tribal ways. Many people around the world appreciate (indeed, prefer) this communal way of life and will defend it from insult. It is not always uncivilized to be tribal. The point is to strike at the awful effects that extreme tribalization can have – to oppose not a terrorist's or insurgent's religion, but the reduction of that religion to raw tribalist tenets."

So, with all of this information in mind, this is what I would like to publically ask our American Supreme Court, "Where do we, as Americans, draw the line between freedom of speech and when freedom of speech - crosses the line - to embrace any detrimental, to society at large, religious-based fundamentalist extremism of any self-association and yes, even Christian self-association?"

And yet as I contemplate on David Ronfeldt's words, "Humiliating insults upset peace more than anything else – reciprocal gift giving is essential - in tribal councils…. It does not tolerate minority rights and dissident views once a consensus emerges – and there are only two ways to restore honor: compensation or revenge – a tribe may view itself as a realm of virtue, but see outsiders as a different realm that may be treated differently, even brutally, especially if they are "different!" – The more that extremists create divisions between "us" and "them," vainly claim sacredness solely for their own ends, demonize others, reveal in codes of revenge, crave territorial and spiritual conquests, and suppress moderates who disagree – all the while claiming to act on behalf of a deity – the more their religious orientation becomes utterly tribal and prone to wreaking violence of the darkest kind,"

… and while personally thinking of David Ronfeldt's words, I FEAR for America's soul.

Then the words, "wreaking violence of the darkest kind" repeat over and over in my mind as I think of all of the labels and words we use to separate and delineate ourselves from one another and by realizing that we use words to demonize our opposition then I see that Satan's favorite tool to use here in America is simply: "any tribe." Yes, America in the 21st century still has primitive warring tribes. Call them liberal or conservative, Christian, Muslim, or Jew, Straight or Gay, Democrat or Republican – heck, what's in a name – "By the fruit you shall know them" and you shall know it to be equally constructive to all or self-destructive to society as a whole – and maybe "by the fruit" that should tell us, all in itself, who is a False believer and who is falsely using religious beliefs to satisfy an agenda all of their own.

But the hardest thought to bear is the conflict of trying to decide: whether it's a tribe called a corporation or a tribe called "my parents" where does society come in to play to pick up the slack when the chains of command are broken down and you, as a lone individual, are stuck in a very "un-kind-tribe" that's cannibalistic and will sacrifice one segment of that society for the enjoyment and enrichment of another segment of that self-same society? And yes Dear God, I really pray for us to know how to counter all self-centered "WRONG LEADER" motivations, we could stop all human pain right now, if only we were willing to just honestly share and listen!

And as I fear that Satan may be destroying America from within her very own shores, by way of seducing her own two political parties, I think more of David Ronsfeldt's words: "Most antagonists, no matter how high-mindedly they proclaim their ideals, are operating in terribly tribal and clannish ways. Some, such as Al Qaeda terrorists, are extreme tribalists who dream of making the West start over at a razed, tribal level."

And then I think to my own self, "Oh my God, isn't that what the Republicans in Congress are trying to do to the health-care bill in America? Don't they want to raze it, and scrap it, and according to the leading Republicans we definitely need to – 'throw it out and just start it all over again'…. Knowing, by their actions and attitudes, the only way they will honor it will be with only their directions and input!"

So while I personally do battle in my mind with the thought of Al Qaeda and American Congressional Republicans scarily sharing the same goal of making America start all over again with "new ideologies," from deep within my mind I hear Satan laugh! And after his mean-spirited laughing he says to me, "See how powerful I am at division – I've now gotten you to hating all Republicans!" But it's at this point I return the laughter and reply, "Satan aren't you forgetting something really important – I DON'T hate all republicans just like all republicans don't hate homosexuals.... I just won't bow down to worship ANY political parties' mantra even with the fact that one of my modern-day heroes is a very caring, sharing, very smart Republican!"

It's then I knock a blow to the devil with a very powerful news article by Jen Christiansen published by PlanetOut and it reads in part, "Former U.S. Senator John Danforth broke ranks with many fellow Republicans over the weekend as he criticized as "silly" the effort to amend the Constitution to ban same-sex marriage.

Danforth, who is now an ordained Episcopal priest, told the crowd of hundreds that the anti-gay amendment was one more sign of how religious conservatives hurt the G.O.P.'s mission. In the past he has called this the "us-vs.-them, my-God-is-bigger-than-your-God, velvet fist variety of Christian evangelism."

"Once before, the Constitution was amended to try to deal with matters of human behavior, that was Prohibition. That was such a flop that it was repealed 13 years later," Danforth said. "Some historian should really look at all of the proposals that have been put forth throughout the history of our country for possible constitutional amendments. Maybe at some point in time there was one that was sillier than this one, but I don't know of one," he said. Danforth said his criticism stemmed from a conservative interpretation of how the country should be governed. "The basic concept of the Republican Party is to interpret the Constitution narrowly, not expansively, so that legislators, and especially state legislatures, can work out over a period of time the social issues of our country," he said.

So I internally debate, the basic Republican concept is to interpret the Constitution narrowly? But I know that the only way to interpret narrowly is to put your mind into a narrow frame and focus of reference, and I wonder, is this what being a True Conservative means, "To always think narrowly?" But I sputter, that's just being "always narrow-minded!" It's then I hear Satan chuckling again and I realize this "us-vs.-them, my-God-is-bigger-than-your-God" type of spiritual warfare isn't over just yet – for any of us!

And with the thought of us all dealing with Velvet-Fisted Christianity, I become even more afraid of all of this ideological-political-tribal warfare going on here in America. So I realize with EXTREMELY DREADFUL FORBODING - we may only be at just the beginning of the end because it's now of utmost importance to bring to the three co-equal branches of our American government's full attention exactly..... "When Religion Becomes Evil."

But then, for me, as all of this information is fully coming into my own awareness, I'm totally confused again because knowing that one of the most important jobs OF government is to protect its citizenry.... what happens when, like a VERY abusive parent - it is the one we have to fully trust and depend on; and yet, thanks to the professional mental therapy that has been provided for me.... I realize that my government is ALSO the very biggest sponsor of "legal" persecutions of me? And from here to the Capital Hill I see so much of Satan's hate shining from sea to sea.

I guess all I can do is now PRAY for my own safety while asking God to deliver me from the evil I see radiating in front of me - that's being directed "straight" toward me - by the very same government I have to rely on for the very protections I need.... And I think, Oh Dear God, what a gargantuan quandary I now find myself most unmercifully trapped in while living in a most UNMERCIFUL "Christian" America!

And I wonder: Is America herself, because of so much collective mean-spirited "KARMA," about to be "drowned in the bathtub" of Satan's UNQUENCHING, un-ending... UNCOMPROMISING... hate?

Once again, only God knows for sure.....

A Hell of a Religious "Tribal Gang"

So while I'm hitting back over the concept of extreme Christian subversion and evil.... I have to admit I've been beaten up pretty badly at times during this Holy War against Homosexuals. But in the past, too many times, along with others throwing jabs and punches, I beat myself up the worst. Yes, guilt is a terrible punishment and burden. Guilt is another ugly animal Satan unleashes for us to carry around inside of our hearts to tarnish our souls. As I personally look within and find that a great guilt is living inside of my own thoughts, I fear. I am made to feel afraid – not just for my soul but also I'm afraid for America's soul. I'm very afraid that when many of us do meet Jesus what will we say if the first thing Jesus has to say is: "You're spiritually bankrupt because you only invested your life's work in the Bernie Madoff school of False Christianity!"?

So, with that fear filled thought I make a great effort to do my own soulful research. Now I understand how powerful thoughts are because thoughts create, for us all, our very own negative and mean-spirited state of mind.

But to counteract that, Jesus reminds me that along with hell.... "Heaven is (also) found within." And so for me to escape my inner hell I have to seek out my own thoughts, attitudes, and motivations. I feel Jesus wants us all to eventually cleans ourselves of thoughts that allow us to take from others while not sharing in return....

So now I must personally purge all thoughts that motivate me to take away from and thereby show a lack of simple respect.

For me, the dark side of the mind that contains hell is an attitude I foster in my mind when I act toward others without common manners. Hell is when I don't mind hurting other people, taking from other people, and it's very easy to curse and think the worst of someone else. That's an attitude that dooms all of us to live our life with hell on Earth!

But, when we are ready, then Jesus shines into our minds with understanding, and peace returns to bless us. To love someone else on earth like Jesus loves us all… no matter what happens or under what conditions… Jesus' priority will always be the extension of LOVE! And pure love is the requirement for the attainment of self inner-heaven.

Again and again Jesus reassures, "I will never leave anyone or forsake anyone." That simple truth is a very powerful thought that calms my mind of my many different fears and my thoughts finally leave hell and return to Grace so then I can express generosity and gratitude to any and everyone. It gives me hope that no matter what other people may say or how they might feel about me – I know I will always have Jesus looking out for me. I will forever say, "I have found Jesus many times deep in my thoughts and he has been there for me when no one else has. Jesus guides me and I know his love. I know his concern for my well being. I know all this because Jesus extends to me such Grace even when I'm at my very worst and I find myself locked in my own mental torment while walking through this valley called the shadow of death.

Then with the kiss of death, creeping up from the back of my mind, I become aware – not of Grace – but un-sympathetic evil. I am now forced to become completely aware of when religion becomes evil not just in my own life but also in the lives of God's other good children.

So to expand on "When Religion Becomes Evil" I read a history book written by Dr. Charles Kimball. He is a professor of religion and chair of the department of religion at Wake Forest University. An ordained Baptist minister who received his Th.D. from Harvard University in comparative religion with specialization in Islamic studies, Dr. Kimball is the author of three books about religion in the Middle East.

It's here I have to thank Jesus for sending me an ordained Baptist minister who has helped me so much in accepting myself as a gay Christian. Dr. Kimball was able to help me so much by writing a book about the conflicts between Islam and Christianity. Therefore he taught me through his book "When Religion Becomes Evil" how to put not just the traditional "War on Terror" but the "Holy War against Homosexuals" into total perspective. In his book Dr. Kimball writes about the five warning signs that tell us, very plainly, when any or all religions are on the verge of becoming – not just dark or dysfunctional but…. Draped in Evil and lacking any civility or the true compassion of the Christ!

It's here I think to myself… is humanities major error, the mistake we keep repeating over and over, the mortal error that we don't do to others as we would have them treat us? Sometimes the simplest words are the most challenging to put into practice. And as the thought of original sin comes up I wonder if the "truly original sin" is just the core sin of believing we're superior? It's when we believe we're superior that Satan can tempt us into believing that God doesn't love - those people - and God's love has to be saved for only the few, the righteous, the holy ones – yes, "those people" who adamantly believe in absolute truth claims!

It strikes me when Dr. Kimball writes: "It is sadly ironic that soldiers in the Army of God intentionally break the commandment not to murder in order to stop people they consider guilty of murder. While truth claims are the essential ingredients of religion, they are also the points at which divergent interpretations arise. When particular understandings become rigidly fixed and uncritically appropriated as absolute truths, well-meaning people can and often do paint themselves into a corner from which they must assume a defensive or even offensive posture. With potentially destructive consequences, people presume to know God, abuse sacred texts, and propagate their particular versions of absolute truth."

So, now I realize by Dr. Kimball's teaching that having "Absolute Truth Claims" is step number one up the ladder of escalation to – When Religion Becomes Evil.

And as I think of absolute truth claims and narrow frames of references, again, I'm reminded of the time I was watching T.V. and the news show reported about everybody in Oklahoma being up in arms because of the Christian/Muslim controversy brought on by the Oklahoma State Representatives who refused to accept, as a gift, the

Holy Qur'an. I do know that many people are taught by many churches that only those people who worship like they do will be saved and enter into heaven. So as I think of absolute truth claims it makes me wonder about all of the churches who now promote ONLY the ideology of select-salvation as an absolute truth claim. Yes, that divisive idea that only a select few will be saved and therefore if someone is different, in any way, they don't deserve to be treated with the same amount of respect that the "saved ones" are. I've personally talked with many evangelical Christians who believe that Muslims, Catholics, and Jews are all evil and will be sent to hell. Of course, I've also met a lot of Christians who do NOT judge and instead they can respect and they honor those people of different faiths and, my God, what a good contrast the love from them makes!

I do know it gave me so much good faith when during the Christian/Muslim debate over the state accepting the Qur'an how many Christians thought it was a wonderful peace offering to extend from those that study Islam. I do know that when those Christian legislators refused the Muslim's gift to the State of Oklahoma it offended not only the Muslim community here but also it offended many parts of the Oklahoma Christian community as well. I just wonder what Jesus sees is at the heart of those governmental representatives' personal motivations that allowed them to disregard the Muslim's gift and instead they slapped Muslims in the face with their very blatant "Christian" disrespect?

I have to strongly say disrespect because after getting educated by Dr. Kimball's book I read, "Jesus is one of the most important and prominent figures in the Qur'an; he is mentioned ninety-three times by name in the sacred scripture of Islam. There is no ambiguity here. Jews, Christians, and Muslims are talking about the same deity. Derogatory proclamations about Islam from prominent Christian leaders in the United States are part of a long history."

Then as I ponder on the concept of "derogatory proclamations" I can relate because I've also personally been on the receiving end of so many "Christian" derogatory statements myself. Now I wonder if "we the people" of the United States have a long history of making the same mistakes over and over again by feeling superior with our personal religious views and beliefs that are erroneously based on absolute truth claims when, in reality, we the people of the United States sometimes don't take the time to get fully educated on the true facts before we jump to a wrong judgment that willfully slaps someone else in the face of their self esteem or self worth? And, the biggest burden for America to carry is if Jesus IS mentioned "93 times by name in the Qur'an" is each attack on the Holiness of the Qur'an as much of an insult to Muslims as Christians are offended when the Holiness of the Bible is not respected? And if Jesus IS a major part of the Qur'an as well as the Bible... is Satan getting Christians to hate Muslims like Satan has gotten some Muslims to hate Christians? Most importantly: Is any attack on the Qur'an or the Bible taken as just one more slap in the face to Jesus Christ himself? Are we STILL crucifying Jesus by proxy when we dare attack someone that Jesus even now deeply loves? Dr. Kimball puts it best when he says: "Rigid truth claims, particularly in times of conflict, are the basis for demonizing and dehumanizing those who differ."

So, as I think of people who demonize and dehumanize, I question if they do those things because it makes them feel superior in a self-inflating perverse kind of way? But that thought makes me nervous because only a real demon knows how to really demonize. Therefore I'm forced to wonder once again, who is the False Christian and who is the True?

I do know it makes me sad that a few Oklahomans felt that the Qur'an would not double the amount of our worldly peace while resting right next to "the gift" called the Bible, especially because if, in gratitude, you open yourself up to the possibility that it has something good to offer with great appreciation it is written in the Holy Qur'an, "There can be no compulsion in matters of religion." (2:256)

This tenet tells us that everyone is responsible and more importantly – able – to find the right path for them to gain peace within. No compulsion means there can and should be – NO fighting, no coercion, no being forced to bow down and worship "absolute truth claims."

Dr. Kimball says: "Religious convictions that become locked into absolute truth claims can easily lead people to see themselves as God's agents. People so embolden are capable of violent and destructive behavior in the name of religion."

So I think more of destructive behavior and I wonder, is that what makes a "Christian" politician take a swipe at another human being for worshiping in the language called Islam? Are those destructive absolute truth claims the same Satan seduced claims that will allow those same representatives to condemn me just because I'm gay – because, in their mind, I'm absolutely gay? Is destructive behavior simply the bottom-line of Satan's manipulation of anyone's core prejudice? God only knows.

Then I worry even more as I read Dr. Kimball's words, "Evangelical Protestants in the west are not the only ones who propagate absolute truth claims. The rise in various forms of fundamentalism around the world is connected to the desire for clarity and guidance in a rapidly changing world. It is much easier to know the truth than to seek it. But religious life is a journey which we learn, unlearn, change, and grow. Religious truths are crucial; they are not easily bottled up or circumscribed by absolutist claims. On the contrary, the pursuit of religious truth is an ongoing process. For Christians, religious education in seminaries and Sunday schools, Bible studies, sermons, and retreats all point to the fact that there is always more to learn, that new information or ways of looking at things is good and healthy. It isn't all set in stone. Even those who devote their lives daily to learning and educating are constantly changing. To illustrate, ask a member of the clergy the following question: Do you ever go back and read your sermons from two or five or ten years ago? How have your views changed? Every clergyperson I know who does this admits it is a humbling discipline. They sometimes happily discover gems or insights that have slipped off the radar screen. More often, they find that continued growth and learning help them frame issues somewhat differently now."

So, after all of Dr. Kimball's wise words on this subject I have to ask, what about all of the people in the world who are proudly carrying around negative absolute truth claims and what can we do when they don't believe they have anything else new to learn? What about those people who have totally narrow frames of focus and because of their "horse-blinders" and tunnel vision they see the issue of continual personal inner growth and learning as too humbling of a discipline to go through? God knows, maybe that's the strongest sign yet that those people may be False Christians just because they "absolutely believe" they all ready know it all and they may be False especially when they believe anyone – not equally perfect to them – will end up going to hell. And what an ego trip, that must be, to feel anyone has the right to condemn someone else to hell.

So, as I fight with myself over the concept of Christian love vs. Christian hate, continue my sometimes painful learning or continuing onward in my "tried and true," set, old ways.... I will say that while all of this religious inner intensity seems to be compounding and I'm getting uncomfortably alert to the oncoming dangers ahead, thank God, I'm finally fully-aware that those people who worship ANY religion that promotes ANY kind of hate is – one hell of a religion – to now try and want to emulate much less share with the world.

And dear God, please help me to NEVER, ever feel like I need to join, for a false ego boost, one of those very numerious .... and dangerous... "religiously superior" Christian Country Club kind of Tribal Church Gangs!!!!

BLIND OBEDIENCE

S tep number two to when religion becomes evil, according to Dr. Kimball,

"This is a pivotal point at which religion often becomes evil. Authentic religion engages the intellect as people wrestle with the mystery of existence and the challenges of living in an imperfect world. Conversely, blind obedience is a sure sign of corrupt religion. Beware of any religious movement that seeks to limit the intellectual freedom and individual integrity of its adherents. When individual believers abdicate personal responsibility and yield to the authority of a charismatic leader or become enslaved to particular ideas or teachings, religion can easily become the framework for violence and destruction... The dangers associated with the lack of intellectual scrutiny toward religious leaders are just as real when it comes to powerful religious ideas or doctrines.... Reading through volumes of "Christian" sermons in support of slavery or apartheid today accents the point. Authentic religion encourages questions and reflection at all levels. When authority figures discourage or disallow honest questions, something is clearly wrong. Doctrinal positions supporting otherwise unethical behavior must always be challenged."

And as I read the words of Dr. Kimball, "When authority figures discourage or disallow honest questions, something is clearly wrong," sadly I am reminded of the spiritual wounds I personally received a number of years ago when inter-reacting with a Southern Baptist pastor and his flock of believers who lived in a quant small town on the outskirts of Plano, Texas. Yes 1996, I remember that distinct church, it

97

was my friend Deanna's church, and I still carry those crucifixion scars to this day.

Ironically, I remember how friendly the people were when first introducing themselves, but, some of the people there at that church knew my secret. Yes, some of those devote Southern Baptists knew that I was gay! And I have to admit they tried their damnedest to share the gospel with me. They very plainly let me know, up front, they were out to save my soul. But we ran into a serious problem when I told them that they wouldn't be able to save me... because I already was.... or so I thought. But those very determined and well meaning people couldn't get past the realization that I was a Christian and a homosexual. So those religiously devout people let me know that, very plainly, there was no way on God's green earth that I could be truly saved... if I'm still gay!

And then to compound insult to injury, at one point when the Baptists were trying their best to get me to repent of "that kind" of sex, I mentioned to one of the church leaders about a tape a friend of mine had given me. The tape is called "Teachings on Love" and it's by a Buddhist monk named Thich Nhat Hanh. The things I learned from being exposed to that Buddhist Monk's instructions has taught me so much about love and good communication skills that I wanted to share it with those people from that small upstanding Texas town. After I heard what the monk had to say with his lessons on love I was able to understand completely why Thich Nhat Hanh had been nominated for the Noble Peace Prize. Yes, this very humble Buddhist monk had been nominated for the Peace Prize by the Rev. Martin Luther King Jr. in 1967 in honor of the monk's lifelong efforts to generate peace and reconciliation for not just Vietnam but also for the whole world. So while Thich Nhat Hanh helped me to understand a lot about life and love and healing, what I failed to understand was the Southern Baptists' fear of anything not in the Southern Baptist image.

Of course, maybe I over loaded them because they weren't really comfortable inter-reacting with a real live gay, but when I talked about what I learned from a Buddhist monk they really freaked-out! Those small town Baptists told me that Buddhism is a cult and that if I listened to a Buddhist I would be mislead. They told me Buddhists worship a false god. So I asked them, "If this tape from a Buddhist monk is so bad for my soul won't you at least take the time to listen to it so that you can tell me exactly what's wrong?" All I got from Thich Nhat Hanh's message was a deeper understanding of compassion and true respect. But, "No!" they said, "We will NOT listen or be miss-lead by a false religion.... You listen to us, there is only One-Way to heaven and that way is "our-way," trust us, only we can really show you how!"

But as I kept telling them I didn't understand their resistance to Buddhism, they of course couldn't seem to understand my resistance to bowing down to worship only their limited and limiting beliefs.

I figured it was around at that point they gave up on trying to be nice, while trying to save my soul, but I must admit that while they, in their eyes, couldn't brag about saving my soul, at that time those small town Southern Baptists were able to teach me a very valuable lesson about love. They taught me about the dangers of how a closed mind leads to a closed heart and they helped teach me a lot about what love isn't! Love, I now know – isn't interested in exerting absolute truth claims or in the blind obedience of its followers.

So as my journey continued, I go from a small town Baptist church to a Buddhist Temple. I just wonder why those Baptists, in a parting shot, said that when I left their church... I was bound and determined to go to hell? But now, with that experience way behind me, I'm bound to ask, "Were they so resistant to exploring Buddhism because of what they would see? Or, dear God was their resistance really all about what they were so afraid they would-not see? Maybe they were really afraid they wouldn't see an honest logical reason to claim Buddhism as a false religion.

So, for me, what a contrast to go to a church that preached of the end times, evil enemies, and having to always hate sin to then go to a Buddhist Temple that doesn't condemn anyone. And what a personal revelation especially after reading Thich Nhat Hanh's book, "Living Buddha Living Christ," in this book the monk writes of all the similarities between Buddhism and Christianity. How enlightening to read a book that unites the two religions instead of capitalizing on exploiting the differences. In Living Buddha Living Christ the book speaks of what it means to try and understand another person's point of view. The book even talks a lot about the Holy Spirit of God and it teaches about the need for forgiveness from all sides of the view. I was most impressed when Thich Nhat Hanh said that in his private home he has an altar with Christ and Buddha, side by side.

Yes, it makes me wonder what Jesus thinks of Thich Nhat Hanh and the fact that a soft-spoken Buddhist monk is able to speak and love in two distinct spiritual languages? Yet, it also makes me wonder what Jesus now thinks of those proud strong-armed Southern Baptists who have a hell of a hard time loving in just one language?

But then, to counter, I think of all of the other Southern Baptists who, in spite of traditional official church policy condemning homosexual love, they are still able to forgive and do not judge – like my friend Deanna who did NOT judge me – at least until the very end when her church ultimately convinced her she had to! So I do wonder: Are Christians who "till death do we part;" yet, still they REFUSE TO JUDGE - are these kinds of worshipers the real True Christians? Because it does seem in our crazy mixed up world there are also two kinds of Baptists, or should I say, "There are really ALL kinds of Baptists?" Especially after I read Dr. Kimball's words, "As a Christian, I look both outside myself and within for light to illuminate the path. I remain a Baptist in the South (which is no longer synonymous with being a Southern Baptist), in part because the tradition affirms individual freedom and responsibility before God. The priesthood of all believers is a foundational tenet of the Baptists and others in the free-church tradition. But danger always lurks nearby. There are few checks and balances for individuals or congregations at this end of the Christian spectrum. Anyone who feels "called" to ministry can be ordained if a recognized church affirms that "call." In this tradition, seminary education is not formally required; the suitability of a person for leadership is not usually tested through a screening process or psychological exam."

And as I now freak out, personally, at the thought of the possibility of mentally unsuitable preachers taking no psychological exams before influencing young and impressionable people.... I read on...... "Individual leaders can and do preach and teach all across the theological spectrum. Take a look around the national scene in the United States and you will readily discover that Baptists are a varied lot. Communal safeguards are built in through committees and congregational decision-making practice. But charismatic leaders often have extraordinary power and influence when there is no presbytery or bishopric to which they are accountable. It is not surprising, therefore, that many Christian cult groups spring from Baptist and Pentecostal churches. Blind obedience is a sure sign of trouble. The likelihood of religion becoming evil is greatly diminished when there is freedom for individual thinking and when honest inquiry is encouraged. As the Buddha lay on his deathbed, he emphasized human responsibility and used the metaphor of light. He offered these poignant final words to his disciples: Do not accept what you hear by report, do not accept tradition, do not accept a statement because it is found in our books, nor because it is the saying of your teacher... Be ye lamps unto yourselves..... Those who, either now or after I am dead, shall rely upon themselves, it is they who shall reach the very top-most height."

And as I read Dr. Kimball's (a kind Baptist preacher) book quoting the Buddha I'm reinforced by the words, "Those who... shall rely upon themselves, it is they who shall reach the very top-most height" And I start to understand how wise both Dr. Charles Kimball and Thich Nhat Hanh are for taking the sometimes lone and principled stand. I understand that's why Thich Nhat Hanh speaks so much about the Holy Spirit in his book "Living Buddha Living Christ" and with Dr. Kimball's great reference to "those who shall rely upon themselves" it helps me to truly "see the greatness of the Holy Sprit's light!"

Holy Bible, John 20:21-22 Again Jesus said, "Peace be with you! As the Father has sent me, I am sending you. And with that he breathed on them and said, 'Receive the Holy Spirit'"

So whether you are a Christian, Muslim, Jew, or even a homosexual Evangelical part Catholic/Buddhist (like I am).... Thank God Jesus is willing to share the Holy Spirit with anyone and everyone. And, upon receiving the Holy Spirit.... we do not need to ever depend on just mankind to approve, inspire, or guild us! Thank God, as time goes by I'm finally learning to trust the Holy Spirit, within me, way more than I can regretfully now trust those False Christians I find, ruining the True Gospel that I find... that SHOULD be totally embracing each and everyone. So, dear God bless the True Christians of the world who refuse to follow blindly and, in return, they will never-ever turn a blind eye to the many good things that are found in far off and unexpected places.

And dear God because False Christians are still my brothers and sisters, please help me to develop a much stronger sense of inner unconditional love – just like Jesus has – so that when persecutors do come knocking in the dark-dead of night, to beat up or torture me, I am still able to fight off the Satan's hate I see, sadly, staring at me within the hearts of my very own fellow family of man. Yes, I now know we're only fighting each other while we are all trapped in this worldly dream created out of the simple belief in an unequal kind of god's love, yes, this hate-filled dream seems to be made from nothing more than an "uncaring god-love" based on some people's blind worshiping... of blind obedience.

The Ideal Time for a Conflict

Step number three onto When Religion Becomes Evil is: Establishing the "Ideal" Time. According to Dr. Kimball, "Among evangelical Christians, premillennial dispensationalism became a dominant interpretive framework during the preceding century. This scheme divides time into defined segments or dispensations, the final one of which is preceded by cataclysmic events. We are thus in a time "before" the final dispensation. Popular preachers and turbulent global events – wars, natural disasters, and famine – helped fuel the notion that the world is fast approaching a seven – year period of great tribulation during which Satan's forces will rule under the leadership of the Antichrist. At the end of this time of great upheaval and suffering, according to this scheme, Jesus will come again to lead the forces of good at the battle of Armageddon. He will then bind the forces of evil and establish his reign in the New Jerusalem before the culmination of human history and the Day of Judgment. Thus proponents warn that the earth is exceedingly close to the tribulation, the end of history as we know it, and the millennial reign."

And as I think of my past traditional evangelical's view of "the end times" this is another very harsh battle I fight with the extreme contrasts that A Course in Miracles now teaches. With what I have gathered from "the Course" the end times should be for us, instead of dreading tribulation, war, and punishment, - the end times are something for us all to look forward to with compassion and total understanding. The end times will precede the second coming of Christ because by the world's different religions finally uniting - as one - they will all teach us to look within our own selves and by us, as individuals, seeing our own capacity to both love and hate the ultimate Armageddon battle we will all fight will be to finally scrutinize our own private personal actions - each one to himself – no more finger pointing – and then we will all eradicate all evil thoughts in our own minds that we personally hold against God by us holding things against our fellow Sisters and Brothers. And as enlightenment eventually comes to us all– so to the love of Jesus Christ will also come and unite with us all!

But now, as I pick up the heavy cross of self-introspection, I re-debate the view of salvation for all vs. select-salvation; and, do I dread the cataclysmic end times or do I look forward to the sanity the end times will bring? Then, with all of these conflicts and contrasts, on top of it all, I get even more confused about all of this when I examine the world-views of a traditional fundamentalist Christian named Pat Robertson.

Learning from Dr. Kimball's... When Religion Becomes Evil, I read, "Pat Robertson embraces a reconstructionist theological position. This orientation challenges the mechanisms of the state and seeks to bring all of life under God's rule.

"For reconstructionists there is no neutral ground, no sphere of activity outside God's rule. One is either following God in all aspects of life or not following God at all. One is either engaged in godly politics or is participating in the anti-God structures that now threaten the home, the school, and the church.... Like their premillennial cousins, reconstructionists wait for a dramatic change in history. But they are not merely waiting." Reconstructionists seek "to remove the political and institutional barriers to God's law in order to impose the rule of God's law" Robertson's approach is well documented... Rather than choosing a top-down political strategy, he organized a grassroots, bottom-up approach under the auspices of the Christian Coalition. With surprisingly little effort, Robertson revealed how small numbers of committed Christians could literally take over school boards and city councils and control Republican precincts in many states.

The political sophistication and rapid success of the Christian Coalition during the first half of the 1990's was stunning. In addition to controlling school boards and city councils, these activists effectively commanded the political power among Republicans in twenty states.

As their positions translated into official planks in party platforms and policies in local school districts, many people and organizations they targeted began to look more closely at the theological underpinnings of Robertson's movement. They didn't have to look long or hard. Robertson's daily television program, The 700 Club, and his books spelled it out; the structures of government and the legal and educational systems were effectively under the dominion of Satan. Complete overhaul was needed to establish God's rule in this land.

"Satan has established certain strongholds. He goes after areas of our society which are crucial. He has gone after the education system and has been very successful in capturing it. He has gone after our legal profession and has been successful, through the ACLU and others, in capturing large portions of the legal system. He's gone after the government and moved it away from the more free enterprise system we've known and turned it into a socialist welfare state. He's gone after the family, the church, etc., with less success, but nevertheless he's battering away. These places control society.... I don't know if Satan has been able to get to the military yet, but he's tried.... Satan hates people. He desires to destroy people.... We need to do spiritual warfare."

Robertson's religious and political battle plan envisioned the Christian Coalition working in tandem with a wide array of church-related community action councils across America. They enjoyed tax-exempt status under section 501 (c) (3) of the IRS code. Such organizations can only direct a small portion of their budgets to political activities. There are limits on participating or intervening in political campaigns, including making statements for or against candidates for public office. These groups did just that through the distribution of millions of thinly disguised "voter guides." The guides rated local, state, and national candidates – often erroneously – for public office on eight or ten hot-button issues. The "guides" were conveniently sized to fit as church bulletin inserts; they were distributed in thousands of churches the Sunday before Tuesday elections. The tactic was highly effective in many instances; it was also blatantly deceitful and probably illegal. Few public officials, however, dared challenge the process in court lest they be seen as somehow beating up on "religious" institutions.

On several occasions I (Dr. Kimball) asked Ralph Reed and other leaders in this movement to explain and clarify how they were not violating the spirit, if not the precise letter, of the law. Were they not deliberately spreading sometimes false and misleading information about candidates in order to influence voters? Did they not actively promote a strategy of running "stealth" candidates, that is, people who deliberately hid their real agenda until after they were elected and in position to change the system? How do these tactics square with responsible Christian witness or tax-exempt status? The responses were predictably weak and couched in legalese. But a deeper message always resided in Robertson's theological statements. He saw the battle in cosmic terms of good and evil. God's rule must prevail against the principalities and powers controlled by Satanic forces. The end, in effect, justified the means... The mixing of God, a narrow understanding of Christianity and country lies at the heart of this powerful movement. Small wonder that Pat Buchanan, another Republican presidential candidate, chose the Christian Coalition's national convention in 1993 to state his position clearly: "Our culture is superior because our religion is Christianity and that is the truth that sets men free." However deeply that view is held by those with an agenda for a Christian America, it appears that a great deal of work remains to be done. Eight years later, in the immediate aftermath of the September 11th attacks, Jerry Falwell appeared on Robertson's 700 Club and revealed....his belief that pagans, abortionists, feminists, and gays and lesbians had helped the attacks happen. Pat Robertson's response to Falwell: 'I totally concur.'"

And as I personally think of Pat Robertson, Pat Buchanan, and Jerry Falwell I have to wonder if these men are the False Christians the Bible warns me off? Are these men False Christians not just because they cause religion to lie down in bed with their own personal worldly-politics; but, are these men False Prophets because they are clearly blatant Christian-hypocrites? It's then I realize how very much more intense these volleys of thought are getting. And now I am very, very troubled.

I am troubled by the notion that Pat Robertson is acting as a "stealth" under the radar "pure capitalist" masquerading Christian when he blatantly promotes the free market system over any redistribution of wealth to help the defenseless poor! Clearly a True Christian understands in Matthew 19:20-23 "All these (laws) I have kept." The young man said. "What do I still lack?" Jesus answered, "If you want to be perfect, go, sell your possessions and give to the poor, and then you will have treasure in heaven. Then come follow me."

When the young man heard this he went away sad, because he had great wealth. Then Jesus said to his disciples, "I tell you the truth, it is hard for a rich man to enter the kingdom of heaven."

And, I'm confused again as the Holy Spirit loudly lectures within me, the Spirit's booming voice tells me, "If that parable is not about Jesus totally embracing taking care of the less fortunate and weak – then I don't know what good True-faith-based Compassion can really do to establish a Heaven on Earth – the kind of Earth that Jesus would WANT to come back to!" So, with my Spirit's financially gifted prodding I question what's up with all of this devious dark-financial worshiping. I do wonder what our world would be like if the True Christians of America spoke up and finally - and just FAIRLY redistributed just enough wealth to the point that no person – not one – is ever left out in the cold to die all alone in poverty and in shame while they die wondering where in this worldly hell are all the True Christians who truly care? Yes, only Jesus knows who really cares about the sick and the poor and only He knows what our world could NOW be like! So as I try to imagine a world Jesus comes back to without ANY "working-class poor" I wonder again if I'm the crazy Christian for wanting to help those who are always knocked down to the ground at the hands of a "pure-capitalist's" sponsorship of the many diverse business laws leading to the unfair financial advantages for the top 1%? Yes, I'm very divided about what to think when the bible tells me to NOT worship the god of mammon yet while I still look about me and see so many "Christians" fighting any kind of logical financial reform, while they loudly protest, "Cut the poor-person's 'entitlements' instead"? And I wonder what so many Christians are going to say on the day Jesus really does show them just how "ENTITLED" they were… instead of the poor? Especially, I debate, when the Bible clearly states to those who "much is given" – much is expected; so I wonder: Why don't all Christians expect Jesus to ask them to demonstrate a more generous financial responsibility that isn't just based on growing their own personal financial portfolios? Then I question if anyone can really be called a True Christian while they are still being seen as to bowing down to only a "free market" system that is based on the "unlimited freedom" to corrupt, capitalize, and exploit – to rape and pillage the poor and uneducated? And in contrast I see they won't simply "tame the beast" that is feeding them and instead they are fighting tooth and nail the right to give every poor working person a break that just makes sure their basic needs are comfortably taken care of – and I see SO many people all around me more upset battling over gay marriage than are fighting for the sanctity of financially fair equality.

So, sadly, in our war against poverty right now it seems the sick and poor have to wait once again, while being forced to fend for themselves, because as Pat Robertson declared, "We need to do spiritual warfare." And as I think of all of the times the Bible warns me to stay away from people who cause divisions.... I'm totally divided by the thought of Pat Buchanan saying, "Our culture is superior because our religion is Christianity." And then I think of the times the Bible says not to be proud or to boast.... And, as I think of "superiority," I wonder if America's favorite brand of National Christianity is to be based on an inclusive or exclusive belief in Christ or hell? Does America embrace everyone into the arms of Christ's salvation or does America think that it is superior, like Pat Buchanan says, because the superior people are saved while the inferior people are not... and to hell with the ones who are not; and as an added monetary bonus: Is it easily justified to take advantage of the ones who are not? So in my mental confusion all I can think of is to pray that a Christianity based on sharing salvation with all... while also taking care of "the whole lot" is a much more superior way to think of others – what a SUPERIOR WAY TO TREAT OTHERS! But then again suddenly, I'm divided by what's to be worldly classified as "True Christianity."

I'm totally divided when I hear that Jerry Falwell revealed in the aftermath of the 9-11 tragedies that, "pagans, abortionists, feminists, gays and lesbians had helped the attacks happen." And Pat Robertson's response to Jerry Falwell's belief, "I totally concur.""

It's then I get totally scared half out of my hell... as my therapists knowledge of projection now comes into my very crippled and crazed consciousness. "Projection is the opposite defense mechanism to identification. We project our own unpleasant feelings onto someone else and blame them for having thoughts that we really have." And then I am forced to think long and hard over Pat Robertson saying, "Satan has established certain strongholds. He goes after areas of our society which are crucial… he has gone after the education system…he has gone after our legal profession…. He's gone after our government….. he's gone after the family, the church…."

And projection again smashes into my mind as I remember that "a projectionist" is "an individual who possesses malicious characteristics, but who is unwilling to perceive himself as an antagonist, convinces himself that his opponent feels and would act the same way."

So, after all of my therapist's wisdoms… I cringe when I see that Pat Robertson very pointedly said, "I don't know if Satan has been able to get to the military yet, but he's tried….Satan hates people. He desires to destroy people,"

And then I think of all of the homosexuals who have had life, liberty, and their personal freedom destroyed by the "Christian Coalition" - all at the hands of many men like Jerry Falwell, Pat Robertson, and Pat Buchanan. So, in respect of the law that teaches us to pray for those people who still like to demonize us while calling us "enemy," - all I can think of now is to say, "God help each and every one of us." Especially after Dr. Kimball says, "Those who narrowly define ideal temporal structures of the state and determine that they are God's agents to establish a theocracy are dangerous. Religion is easily corrupted in this context. Beware of people and groups whose political blueprint is based on a mandate from heaven that depends on human beings to implement."

But as I'm now reaching the last straw of my sanity when I again reread Dr. Kimball's recommendation that "those who narrowly define ideal temporal structures of the state and determine that they are God's agents to establish a theocracy are dangerous" yes, I scream in pain as I keep zeroing in on the words, "those who narrowly define…" because I am again reminded of those strict Republican pure Federalist Constitutionalists who worship the idea that the only perfect world is a world full of only their OWN "strictly-narrow-minded world views."

But then the Holy Spirit gives me hope because IF God CAN save everybody that means even Pat Robertson, Jerry Falwell, and Pat

Buchanan will eventually be saved even if God has to save them from their overbearing, overblown, own sense of superiority!

And then Satan tempts me, with all he's got, into hating these very men while he's pointing out the fact that these very rich white men "are the perfect roll-models" to teach the world how to really break out into a fight over who thinks who is the most relevant, smartest, and oh so important!"

So, I pray to God that the Holy Spirit can now soften my heart to help me to understand that like these men, yes, even I have at times made mistakes out of blind ignorance. I have to forgive myself as well as them; yes, I too have invested unwisely in the world at times. But, thank God, I finally know that I don't have to let those "Christian" men continue to spiritually beat me up for "my sin" of homosexuality because, thanks to my Holy Spirit, I now know perfectly Pure-Capitalist-Christians are also just everyday common sinners... because, by their actions, they sometimes seem to forget, "A man's soul's worth is NEVER to be based on worldly possessions." Yes, dear God, each one of us, it seems, share equality in our own common ability to court physical or material weaknesses.

THE END JUSTIFIES ANY MEANS

S tep number four causes the tension and terror level to rise sharply. Step number four: to When Religion Becomes Evil is when "the end justifies any means." Dr. Kimball writes: "When a key feature of religion is elevated and in effect becomes an end, some people within the religion become consumed with protecting or achieving that end. In such cases, that component of religion functions like an absolute truth claim, and zealous believers become blind in their single-minded defense of it. As we will see, this corruption takes many forms, but the pattern is unmistakable. The end goal of protecting or defending a key component of religion is often used to justify any means necessary. The most obvious sign of this corruption is visible when compassionate and constructive relationships with others are discarded.... Regrettably, corruption of religion in the context of protecting or defending something considered sacred is all too common."

So as I try to mentally process these words of Dr. Kimball I flash on the idea that to False Christians, "the end goal of protecting or defending a key component of Christianity is often used to justify any means necessary." And with that concept, I now get a mental glimpse into the inner-workings of the mind of a serial-hypocrite. Yes, a serial-hypocrite who can cast stones at other people all the while without seeing the sins of their very own. A serial-hypocrite who becomes totally blind in their single-minded defense of the laws they personally choose to address, prioritize, and enforce – as Satan convinces them that they have total impunity and can escape from the very "trap of the law" they hold others to.

111

James 2:8-13 "If you really keep the royal law found in Scripture, 'Love your neighbor as yourself" you are doing right. But if you show favoritism, you sin and are convicted by the law as lawbreakers. For whoever keeps the whole law and yet stumbles at just one point is guilty of breaking – ALL OF IT. Speak and act as those who are going to be judged by the law that gives freedom because judgment without mercy will be shown to anyone who has not been merciful. – Mercy triumphs over judgment."

And as I think of the words, "If you show favoritism, you sin" I think of all of the people who now profess to be strictly Christian and yet there is so much "Christian" favoritism to be found here in America. And so I ask Jesus "Is this what the Religious Right is doing when it is now caught up in a fight to the finish over the issue of the sanctity and sacredness of straight-marriage? In Jesus' eyes I wonder: is the Religious Right guilty of showing exclusive favoritism toward their own very religiously-straight selves? And as I think of the words, "Love your neighbor as yourself" I wonder how the Religious Right can even dare to refuse to allow gays and lesbians the right to marry when I know – sure as hell – the Religious Right wouldn't want America to pass a law outlawing straight-marriage on the grounds that with the divorce rate as high as it is – the sanctity of marriage needs to be protected from "those kinds of straights"....

So I am put on a code-red battle-alert as I read an article that tells me, "Baptist divorce rate higher than average." This is according to the Baptist Standard, and this is from an article written by Ken Camp of Texas Baptist Communication, with additional reporting by RNS

""Born-again" Christians are more likely to go through a marital split than are non-Christians, according to a new study by the Barna Research Group." Using statistics drawn from a nationwide survey of nearly 4,000 adults the Barna data show 11 percent of the adult population is currently divorced but that 25 percent of all adults have experienced at least one divorce. Among "born-again" Christians 27 percent currently are divorced or previously have been divorced, compared with 24 percent among adults who are not "born-again" Surprisingly, the Barna report said, the Christian group whose adherents have the highest likelihood of getting divorced are Baptists. The only group to surpass Baptists were Christians associated with non-denominational Protestant churches."

And then as I think of the statistics that show 11 percent of the adult population is currently divorced but that 25 percent of all adults, and 27 percent of "born-agains" have experienced at least one divorce – I go a little more crazy when I contrast those percentages with the fact that homosexuals are estimated to be only 10 percent of the whole human population. So logically, the true fact is that there are currently more divorced straight adults in America than there are estimated to be the total number of gays and lesbians combined. And as I think of the even smaller percent of the 10 percent of those gays and lesbians who now just want to get married – and yet the leaders of many of America's Christian churches still demonize and criticize any same-sex union. Yes, they prioritize, they organize, they tell us how to vote all while some Charismatic leaders proudly point their fingers and preach to us of exclusion, superiority, and what "the law" now says.

Galatians 3:10-11 "All who rely on observing the law are under a curse, for it is written "Cursed is everyone who does not continue to do everything written in the "Book of the Law" clearly no one is justified before God by the law because "The righteous will live by faith." And I do personally have faith in Ephesians 2:8-9 "For it is by grace you have been saved, through faith – and this is not from yourselves, it is the gift of God – Not by works, so that no one can boast."

So regrettably I'm cornered in the corral over the fact that no True Christian is supposed to boast and yet, so much "Christian" boasting is now going on over how many people "they have personally converted and saved" while also boasting about how hard they are working to "protect the sanctity of marriage!"

1 John 1:8-10 "If we claim to be without sin, we deceive ourselves and the truth is not in us… If we claim we have not sinned, we make him out to be a liar and his word has no place in our lives."

And as I think of people who act like they have never committed a sin against "the Law" and people who are serial-hypocrites and tried and true homo-haters I realize how being on step number four continuing up the ladder to When Religion Becomes Evil is really starting to cause my internal level of stress and anxiety to rise, so I decide I need to spend some quiet time and now appreciate all the wonderful straight friends of mine who told me personally – not only do they support gay marriage – but they support my quest to find my soul-mate and I can definitely count on them to be there and dance at my gay wedding! So I wonder if friends who stand up for you are the "straightest" kinds of friends to have – because it's when the storms rage that you can always count on those True Christians to head straight to your side to share with you your joys and your pains....

But now I am unexpectedly side-swiped by the demon of favoritism again while I wonder if even showing favoritism toward those who practice the Christian faith is a mortal sin. Yes, as Dr. Kimball said, "Muslims, Jews and Christians are all worshiping the very same God," so logic tells me that Islam, Judaism, and Christianity should all be respected as different but equally valuable roads to understanding the One God. One road is no better than the other – yes, I think, God's point is to see to it that we all just arrive at the same destination!

So I wonder if when I hear so many Christians talk about how superior they think their Christian religion is, do they really think Jesus is impressed when they put down other religions at the expense of being able to put their own views of Christianity on a "Cultural-Warrior's" pedestal? And then like a beacon shinning thru the dark, the words of Jesus in John 5:41 keep repeating in my mind, "I do not accept praise from men." And as it goes around and around it repeats, "I do not accept praise from men." And then I worship Jesus because he tells me he doesn't have a "human ego" for me to be forced to bow down to. And out of respect I willingly bow down and praise Jesus because he loves those who practice Islam in total peace - and Jesus loves those who practice Judaism extending it in love, - and Jesus loves those who preach that True Christianity is based on inner-self-security – and I really know Jesus loves it - when he doesn't have to stress to us, "Do not attack."

And then abruptly my thoughts are pulled into the near past....

I am reminded of the time I was watching educational television one night and a program came on about Israel's withdrawal from the Gaza Strip. It was up to the Israeli Police Force to see to it that the government's order of evacuation of the Jewish settlers from Gaza became a reality. The dead-line was fast approaching and Israel's internal police were being mentally prepared to go into the last remaining homes and synagogues to escort the protesters and holdouts onto buses readied for settler transport. The Gaza settlers were being forced from their homes and places of worship because the government of Israel had decided to give an offering of peace to the Palestinian people. Israel in an effort to establish peace in the Middle-East was transferring the land rights of a very beautiful part of God's creation as a show of respect. It seems Israel was trying to show God's other children; and yes, even the whole world – the fact that Judaism is about a religion that teaches its followers to share and take care of others.

But as the I.P.F. was being briefed you could tell by their expressions that they were all having very mixed feelings within the minds of the different police officers. These professional women and men had the extremely hard task of evicting and removing their own people from homes that many were even born in. For many of the evacuees surrendering their homes was not their decision, nor their desire. Middle-East peace or no peace, the remaining Gaza settlers only focused on the fact that they were about to lose their home, identity, and for what, only to face a future full of unknowns? I can relate, I've been forced to move before and it's hard wondering where will I go, who will be my new neighbors? Will I ultimately be happy for the move or will I curse God above for what was taken – taken sometimes from all of us without even leaving any of us any kind of human dignity, while slamming the door and saying, "So go now – get out!" And so many of the evacuees reacted with being treated in that exact vein of thought and feeling like they didn't have a say and adding insult to their injury, the Gaza settlers retaliated in very visible anger.

When the Israeli Police Force finally came knocking door to door many of the Jewish settlers cursed and damned their very own police. Yes, in anger, they reacted out of fear and pain. Many of the refugees had to be literally dragged while kicking and screaming.... Resisting all the way to the waiting buses, it was surely something sad to see. So many settlers threw bottles and stones in retaliation as they showered their inner-frustrations upon the I. P. F. for doing what the settlers thought of as being so unpatriotic. You could tell the refugees were in pain as they kept saying to their own police, "You are a Jew and I am a Jew, so how can you now do what you do to me?"

It's at this point I started to break down myself and I cried. I guess it's because a like experience can pull people together and I personally, right there, related to what those Jewish people were going through. I guess it takes being told to leave – in no uncertain terms – that teaches some of us true humility and compassion.

But with a flash of enlightenment my consciousness moved beyond myself and I realized that I was crying not for the evacuees but my respect was now all wrapped up with the Israeli Police Force. How can I say what that situation taught me; yes, it's so much about a Christ-kind of love! Truly, the women and men of the I.P.F. did such a professional job. But they also did their job with so much more... they did it with compassion, care, and understanding.

The commanders in charge kept telling their officers, "Do not take anything personally – but most importantly – do not attack in return!" With the Jewish settlers feeling hurt the natural tendency was for them to hurt back in return. So many settlers questioned how their own people could evict them. They made the police force feel bad for what they were doing. Many officers on the police force struggled, the hardest, at keeping their own tears from flowing. But the Israeli Police Force knew that what they were doing, while temporarily hurting some people, the I.P.F. knew their efforts would go into a far greater peace effort that would affect the lives of so many more. This Middle-East peace effort was needed because too many innocent people on both sides have been hurt for far too long.

But, as I watched the many settlers throwing objects and hurling insults at their own police at that moment all that would go through my mind was the thought of: "Was this what Jesus went through when he was crucified by God's sometimes ignorant children?" Was the Holy Spirit whispering in Jesus' inner-ear, "Do not attack in return?" By Jesus' actions he didn't return the hate, and now, I see, neither was the I.P.F. But as I watched the Israeli police sometimes crack under the strain and breakdown emotionally, they showed their true humanity. As I watched the I.P.F. give strength and support in return for the bitter hate coming at them from every direction within their own tribe, I was so impressed while they bravely shared in the suffering of their own people. As I watched the Israeli Police Force shed at times their own personal tears I realized right then and there that God had used that situation to not only help bring a little temporary peace to the Middle-East but by extending that peace around the world for all of humanity to see, their peace offering came also to land on me! I was so stunned, in so many ways, but then I truly understood that God had used that important effort by worshipers of Judaism to teach me, a gay male Christian, what it means to be a True Christian – "Christian" not professed by words but with deeds. Those Jewish women and men of the I.P.F. were so very "Christ-like" in the love they could still show and extend to other people when they themselves were being bombarded by so much hatred and contempt.

And I think how ironic that God used a show on P.B.S. about the Israeli and Palestinian conflict to teach me how to extend better understanding to those who so often call us "God-damned traitors!"

Yes, my God loves me and I can feel His Angels watching over me and even when people call me just an "unrepentant-sinner" and treat me with such disrespect I now have the example of God's Jewish Children to thank for teaching me how to give love back in return for the hate sometimes given to us by our very own family.

And may God Bless the Israeli Police Force for giving the whole world a True example worthy enough for all of us to forever now follow, "Remember…. do NOT take anything personal…. and do NOT attack in return!"

So as I repeat those very powerful words and try to put myself in a better frame of reference a pressing thought comes into to view as I read Dr. Kimball's admonition, "Institutional structures develop to meet and serve real needs – religious, political, economic, military, recreational, and so on. As needs change, so too, must institutional structures. This often does not happen easily. Rather than being a means to an end, protecting the religious institution sometimes becomes the end that justifies any means. When this corruption occurs, negative consequences are sure to follow."

Now realizing my future peace and stability are possibly coming into question again I feel a shiver of religious terror run up and down my spine as I try to focus on the hell-fire and damnation I see staring at me, dead – straight ahead.

And as I hear the following satanic words, "Don't be too quick to elevate your Jewish family members to such a high place and calling, remember the Jewish/Palestinian conflict is yet still breathing bitter life to dissentions on all sides of the argument all around the world!"

It's then I realize the major battles over warring tribes won't be over for good until everyone has learned the ultimate fact of a governmentally declared war fought over national pride, national land, or the "sacredness of straight marriage": Yes, all sides are doomed to lose whenever Satan gets the opportunity to play legally "no accountability" free-rein!

But finally, after feeling so lost, for so long, in the flood of Satan's blood lust, I remember the healing words of the Comforter's hymn, "Holy Spirit rain down, rain down" … and so I pray the Holy Spirit now rains down on us all to counter the many times Satan's Hate "reins – down" on a world full of bigotry and extremely "superior" ego-pride!

DECLARING HOLY WAR

A warning to all: this is as bloody bad as it gets because step number five to total escalation of When Religion Becomes Evil is: "Declaring Holy War" Dr. Kimball writes, "… the pattern is unmistakable: wars all over the world are being framed by and fought with reference to religious worldviews… more wars have been waged, more people killed, and more evil perpetrated in the name of religion than by any other institutional force in human history. The sad truth continues in our present day. In somewhat different ways, leaders and combatants continue to depict their war as a holy cause. In doing so, they compound the grave mistakes of those who went before them, and they distort the very heart of the religion they claim to be defending. Declaring war "holy" is a sure sign of corrupt religion. In fact, at the center of authentic religion one – always – finds the promise of peace, both an inner peace for the adherent and a requirement to seek peaceful coexistence with the rest of creation.

Both Christians and Muslims claim that peace lies at the heart of their religions. Both Christianity and Islam, however, have a long and checkered history in which their respective adherents fought for causes declared holy. Many of those conflicts, moreover, involved fighting each other. Not only are these the two largest and most geographically dispersed religious communities; they also head the list of those who have corrupted the heart of their religion by linking it confidently to war. How did this happen? What can be done to stop and reverse the self-righteous march toward destruction?"

And then I praise God because after reading Dr. Kimball's last words I realize I'm not the only one who wants answers to those two very direct questions. "How did this happen?" Well, from all of this hell on earth the Holy Spirit tells me that, again, Satan has been able to use some very powerful peoples' human egos against us all and by some people - teaching us - to deny seeing the "holiness" of each other, Satan has convinced many humans that only "real war" should be considered a truly "holy-way" to win a proud man's salvation. And therefore by seducing some very "respectable" people into cursing and condemning other less "respectable" people - we in essence, all fall in line, to condemn ourselves. But what's worse, then by twisting the sick combo of guilt and hate we all feel inside, to his advantage, Satan gets us to project our own inner frustrations and hatred outward to otherwise innocent people. And I wonder could it be that we ALL just feel so internally bad inside for not living up to the loving standard that God has set for us, by Jesus' very examples? Did God hardwire us ALL, at our core-being, to be exact spiritual copies of "the Christ?" Are we ALL only true to ourselves only when we emulate the love of "the Christ?" Yet, I do believe Jesus is a very hard act to follow especially while we are constantly fighting over who gets to play and win "I have a superior-religion!" And because some people simply don't leave to God the things of God…. we fight and quarrel with our own "family of man" over what we perceive in our eyes makes us better than them. And the more we fight over who is better… the bitter we get and the next thing you know we're all caught up in a very unconscious viscous cycle; thus, our many different Holy Wars continue on only with Satan's encouragement and prodding of the many diverse and religiously-proud-to-parade yet oh so delicate human egos….

And as I've been regularly told, the devil's always in the details…. I read again from When Religion Becomes Evil, "When particular conceptualizations lead to rigid doctrine and cocksure certainty about God, the likelihood of major problems increases rapidly. We have seen this played out with unsettling frequencies as various, often self-appointed, religious leaders boldly speak for God. In the aftermath of the Sept. 11th tragedies several prominent, media-savvy Christian clergy felt compelled to expose publicly the evil nature of Islam. Jerry Falwell, Pat Robertson, and Franklin Graham, the son of Billy Graham, were among the most visible. Not content simply to proclaim the truth of their understanding of Christianity, at different times and in slightly different ways each of these men attacked Islam as a false religion and declared that Allah was a false God. These assaults were terribly divisive, particularly at a time when President Bush and other political leaders were joining voices with many Jewish, Christian, and Muslim religious leaders to strengthen all people of goodwill in collective efforts against violent extremists who claim to be inspired by their religion. In addition, Falwell, Robertson, and Graham revealed their ignorance."

So now I truly debate, maybe Jerry Falwell, Pat Robertson, and Franklin Graham haven't just revealed their ignorance about Islam? Since I have heard they preach negatively toward other religions, combined with their use of all of their many "fear-based facts," by contrasting their personal beliefs on Christianity with the truly loving knowledge about universal salvation maybe these "Christian Leaders" have now mostly revealed their ignorance about what extending True Grace to others really means? And, of course, if these men are "guilty of PROJECTING" maybe when they say, "Islam is a false religion" and they declare that "Allah is a false god" maybe these preachers have unconsciously revealed that they are the only ones "truly false," and I wonder: Maybe Satan has convinced these popular preachers that "a false grace" is something that you can buy from God only by craftily paying your dues through those acts of faith that are only done in front of men – to be seen by men? So, with me now logically stating, "I refuse to believe in their personal religious hate-mongering," I suddenly hear Satan screech at the top of his voice…. I'm just not sure if it's from the pain of me finally not supporting these preachers' ungracious beliefs - or is that screech Satan's laughter about how "those in power" are not supporting my beliefs? My God, who knows? So I'm forced to once again debate more intently.

Yet, in my mind, with those very worldly and powerful preachers now about to be on the receiving end of harsh "biblical quotes" do you think that if half the Christians in the world got up in front of Jerry Falwell, Pat Robertson, and Franklin Graham and called them self-righteous hypocrites who were bound to go to hell by the very laws that they use to condemn anyone not like themselves… well, would that hurt their feelings and self-esteem like it hurts so many homosexuals, or

Muslims, or Jews, or Atheists to be called morally wrong and responsible for 9/11? I honestly wonder if it would hurt those preachers' feelings to condemn them with the same amount of gusto that they condemn other people for worshiping, or not visually worshiping, or for simply loving in a different language? Do these men even care what anyone else thinks? More importantly do they even - really care - what Jesus thinks? Or, are these powerful preachers and their proud followers just using "God's word" to make a quick easy buck, here and there, while people just like them are really only wanting to worship those proud moments as the current "centers of universal attention" because they're now so '"morally perfect?" So, I question, would it truly hurt Jerry Falwell, Pat Robertson, and Franklin Graham if more and more people - woke up - to what's truly going on and started to call them blind "False Christians" while quoting and dedicated to them Galatians 5:7 "You were running a good race, who cut in on you and kept you from obeying the truth?" And the truth is: 1 Timothy 6-5 "If anyone teaches false doctrines and does not agree to the sound instruction of our Lord Jesus Christ and to godly teaching he is conceited and understands nothing. He has an unhealthy interest in controversies and quarrels about words that result in envy, strife, malicious talk, evil suspicions, and constant friction between men of corrupt mind, who have been robbed of the truth and who think that godliness is a means to financial gain." And I honestly wonder if these men and their followers would ever take a stab at worshiping TRULY-DEEP inner-self-reflections? Yes, I personally ponder if they truly have the SELF-COURAGE that's required to really look – DEEP WITHIN THEMSELVES AT THEIR OWN PERSONAL MOTIVATIONS? God only knows....

Then as I internally fight with - faith or observance of the Law - I read, Galatians 3:2-5 "I would like to learn one thing from you: Did you receive the Spirit by observing the law, or by believing what you heard? ARE you so foolish? After beginning with the Spirit, are you now trying to attain your goal by human effort? Have you suffered so much for nothing? Does God give you his Spirit and work miracles among you because you observe the law, or because you believe what you heard?"

I just know I've heard time and again: God gives free grace to those who are willing to share it and out of their internal gratitude they pass it along equally to everyone with – no exceptions. But then I soon have to fight with the idea that to different people there are different kinds of grace and different forms of hell. There are just as many versions of heaven as there are versions of people. And God knows all the ways to perceive finding worldly salvation so I fight with myself about what is classified as biblically wrong and who are really the ones worshiping a False Image of god? And then to make my inner-confusion even more disturbing I read, 1 Timothy 1:3-7 "... so that you may command certain men not to teach false (Christian) doctrine any longer nor to devote themselves to myths and endless genealogies. These promote controversies rather that God's work – which is by faith. The goal of this command is love, which comes from a pure heart and a good conscience and a sincere faith. Some have wandered away from these and turned to meaningless talk. The want to be - teachers of the law, - but they do not know what they are talking about or what they so confidently affirm."

And the greatest battle I've yet to fight is the battle of whether Jerry Falwell, Pat Robertson, and Franklin Graham are the REAL False Prophets the Bible warns me of, time and again, to stay far away from? And as I think of these three very charismatic men I'm again - totally divided... so I wonder even more now because when it does come down to Christianity Vs. Islam are both religions saying the same things through different past holy men? I look at the fact that Jesus is one of the most important and prominent men in the Holy Bible AND the Holy Qur'an so, in reality, is the prophet Muhammad really to be treated with no less respect than Christianities' prophet John the Baptist? And it makes me sad that, right now, Satan is able to get so many people worked up over fighting just about "words" and who is to be considered "Number One!" And I ponder, is number one, in the ways of the world, always "the One" with the biggest human ego? Then I remember, Jesus came - TO serve his fellow man NOT sell his fellow man into the bondage of "servitude" to only "our laws and beliefs."

So as I look at the two faces of Christianity, the False vs. the True, I wonder: How deep is the line drawn between being an extremely humble or extremely prideful, extremely forgiving or extremely judgmental, kind of Christian? I have to wonder about the very word - EXTREMIST - because what do you call a preacher that teaches that different religions, different worshipers, different sexual orientations are all evil and thereby wrong and therefore "different" people only deserve to be met with more war? Are preachers like these considered heroes or hell-raisers? Then I think of how EXREMELY EDUCATED Dr. Kimball is....

So, on the opposite side of the religious spectrum, what would you call a preacher who teaches that God is an all-inclusive Father and that everyone is loved and worthy of forgiveness and salvation while it's all justified by whatever "holy-book" you choose to believe you need to use to understand? And so I reflect: One day will the whole world finally start to grasp the True Power that's behind seeing such dynamic Christian contrasts? I do wonder what the answer would be if I asked everyone this question: "Would you think ultimate salvation for all is an extreme point of view taken only by certified religious extremists? Or, in reality, are preachers that teach Grace belongs to all are these people the most Christ-like of all? I just know through my own personal experience God – the Father – is EXTREMELY LOVING AND TOTALLY FORGIVING and I see him trying to be EXTREMELY GENEROUS – to All His many People!

And as my mind finally returns to thoughts of peace, I focus on the lessons of humility and true understanding that Philip Gulley and James Mulholland teach. And I think of the powers of non-violent Buddhists like Thich Nhat Hanh who want to try to share with us how to, in our civil war kind of world, counter such strong binding and blinding hate. And I think about Dr. Charles Kimball and I wonder if he will now be considered to be the world's number one extremist preacher because he's willing to stand up to "the traditional church" and say the words, "We all still have so much more to now learn!"

Even if that means we have to learn the painful extent to which any religion – even our own dearly beloved Christianity – can be subverted and corrupted – evil in its own right seduced in the night by Satan who so often catches us sleeping....

So to keep from sleeping... I retrace everything I've just learned as my mind trails back to Dr. Kimball's second important question: "What can be done to stop and reverse the self-righteous march to destruction?" And suddenly the Holy Spirit shares its satirical sense of humor when I hear the answer, "That's easy – we just need to get everyone - to only preach about - "just say NO-MORE" to all of this ungodly self-righteousness!"

And in hearing the Holy Spirit's answer I get puzzled again and wonder if my Spirit was really being flippant or in that statement's unmistakable simplicity is it so totally hitting the Oklahoma Bulls-eye TRUTH? God only knows....

My State of War

Well, after finally leaving Dr. Kimball's most dangerous, destructive, rung up the ladder to "When Religion Becomes Evil..." it's time that I try to comprehend the full ramifications of being surrounded and out manned while tied up an Oklahoma political prisoner in a Cultural Warrior's piously declared Holy War. So I guess it's also a good time for me to question if it's by no accident of destiny that I find myself bound-up to living, AND LEARNING, at the ground zero of this unholy, unhappy, Bible Belt War. Therefore, I guess it's only understandable that, with the human cost of war, what little peace of mind I may have had left is to be fractured into separate and very non-equal sections once again.... As I now read the Republican "Grassroots" Party Platform.

The Oklahoma Republican Party Grassroots Platform 2005

1. Family A. Marriage, children, and adoption.

   #3. We support Federal and State legislation that prohibits recognition of same-gender marriages or domestic partnerships.

   #5. We believe that in order to encourage and protect family values, those promoting homosexuality or other aberrant lifestyles should not be allowed to hold responsible positions over children or other vulnerable persons.

   #9. We support adoption only by traditional families or qualified relatives.

E. General

#2. We oppose the promotion of homosexuality, the elimination of laws against sodomy, and the granting of minority protection or special status to any person based upon sexual preference or lifestyle choices.

#3. We believe that homosexuality is not a genetic trait, but a chosen lifestyle.

Curriculum

#7a. Neither homosexual or extramarital sexual activity shall be presented as safe, nor shall they be presented as morally or socially acceptable behaviors.

#9. We oppose the portrayal of homosexual or promiscuous behavior in a positive light in public schools.

II. State, Crime and Punishment

#4. We oppose all hate crimes laws.

IV. Federal
1. Federal General, we support:

#17. Abolishment of hate crime laws. All crimes are wrong and shall be prosecuted accordingly regardless of the race, color, or creed of the victim(s) or the accused.

I take notice that, along with throwing homosexuality into the barrel of all kinds of disgusting traits, in the "abolishment of hate crimes laws" race, color, or creed of the victims is acknowledged. I just wonder when are conservative republicans going to acknowledge that homosexuals can be and currently ARE religious-persecution victims? Will their personal acknowledgment happen only when they themselves also realize that they have been seen - by Jesus - as to being spiritually abusive? And yes all of this hurts everyone, but those Republican Party Platform choices of words may be considered to be "just words" but those words really do hurt us all as good people of good faith and I wonder where is the justice to be found in that declaration of republican "just words?"

And since State Rep. Sally Kern stated that there is "an imaginary wall" between church and state – I guess their grassroots platform lets me know exactly where I stand as a gay male Christian, at least, in the eyes of the Republican Party in this religiously ideological fighting zone called Oklahoma.

But if those Republican Platform words didn't cut deep enough then I hear of the words expressed personally by Rep. Sally Kern... and this is all going on while the ram's horn blasts the call for us to take up arms and go on bullying - on ahead! These forthcoming words are from a newspaper article printed in the Daily Oklahoman, it was written by Michael McNutt featuring quotes by self-avowed Cultural Warrior and Oklahoma State Rep. Sally Kern saying, "The homosexual agenda is destroying this nation; it's just a fact." ... "I honestly think it's the biggest threat our nation has, even more so than terrorism or Islam."

On the audio clipping, Kern can be heard saying the homosexual lifestyle "has deadly consequences for those people involved in it. It is not a lifestyle that is good for this nation. No society that has totally embraced homosexuality has lasted more than, you know, a few decades."

Kern said she made the comments in January to a Republican club meeting away from the state Capital, Kern, a former social studies teacher in the Oklahoma City School District, said she talked about efforts by gay rights groups to target conservatives in recent elections. "I said nothing that was not true, I said nothing out of hate and I don't believe my colleagues will censure me," Kern said. "I was speaking about the homosexual activists who are aggressively funding pro-homosexual candidates against conservative Republicans. In 2006, they targeted conservatives across the nation, mostly at the state and local levels. They took out 50 of them."

And as I read her statement that "they took out 50 of them" I realize how much more complex and personal the in-fighting in this Holy War has become, my condolences to everyone's families.

But I can't help and think does the term "pro-homosexual candidates" equate to the fact that they are candidates who promote the teachings of doctors, therapists, and thoughtful men and women of education who all explain that homosexuality is nothing to be afraid of? Yes, homosexuality is just a normal, harmless, variation found within nature, and NO homosexuality is NOT of the devil!

I just wonder when all of society will acknowledge the fact that homosexuality is to sex what being left-handed is to the brain? Are we now fighting and quarreling over simply - which side of the debate - are people's brains wired?

I do know that it's also very challenging to be "a lefty" while living in this right side dominated world. And, of course, at one point in time it was also traditional church practice to condemn all left handed people by preaching that those people who use their left hand are under the spell and mark of the devil – "they are not normal" And, naturally (?) then some of those people were, in the past, even burned alive for being bewitched. Yes, worldly realities, and what some people will do to other people, can sometimes be "naturally ugly."

So now, I can't help but to wonder who really are the ones unwittingly caught up in Satan's seductive spell of crying - look there's another sacrificial sheep for us to devour? Is that what conservative Christians are doing every time they refer to Muslims or homosexuals as "those ungodly people?"

Especially I wonder about all of this when I read the Holy Bible Galatians 5:13-15

"You, my brothers, were called to be free. But do not use your freedom to indulge the sinful nature (found only through acts of condemnation); rather, serve one another in love. The entire law is summed up in a single command: "Love your neighbor as yourself." If you keep on biting and devouring each other, watch out or you will be destroyed by each other."

And to me, this is the saddest part of this Holy War on top of Holy War, "If you keep on biting and devouring each other... like wolves we will be destroyed by each other."

And I'm now forced to think long and hard on the worry that maybe Satan is winning after all. In the State of Oklahoma is Satan really winning at separating us all from one another during this tragically damning Holy War of All Kinds of Terrors?"

Yes, those ungodly-terrors of not just having to acknowledge the existence and rights of homosexuals; but also, so many people feel the stark terrors of having to respect anyone with a different religion or set of beliefs. This I grasp as I read on March 12th a Daily Oklahoman article by Devona Walker titled, "Do comments create an environment of hate?"

"Sally Kern's comments were not only ignorant but very hurtful," said Jerry Fine, a gay airman who served in Afghanistan. "We need protection from our enemies abroad. We also need protection from within, from people like Sally Kern."

"Kern's critics say her actions have helped create an environment of hate, where crimes such as Domer's killing are perpetrated. (Stephen Domer was a 62 year old gay man who was murdered in a Matthew Shepard hate crime type of seduction of trust followed by Domer being beaten to death at the hands of two white supremacists here in OKC)

"These words are hateful words and can result in hateful actions. This is about responsibility and accountability for words not freedom of expression." Said Richard Ogden, chairman of Oklahoma City – based Cimarron Alliance. Ogden went on to admonish House Speaker Chris Benge, R – Tulsa, for not censuring Kern for her comments. He also lashed out at the Oklahoma Legislature in general for burying four hate-crime proposals in subcommittees, and not allowing them to be debated and voted upon.

Ogden said his group conducted a poll in 2006 that indicated that more than 70 percent of Oklahomans polled believe hate crime laws should include protections for people based on sexual orientation. However, numerous attempts to get bills passed through the Legislature have been unsuccessful.

"Anyone who remains silent is sending the message to the heartland… to gays and Muslims, you are not welcome."

Rep. Al Lindley has worked with Kern, and says he has long suspected she was capable of such views based upon the type of legislation she has proposed. "About once or twice a year, she introduced legislation targeting homosexuals." Lindley, D – Oklahoma City, said. "But I never thought she would say these things publically."

Lindley is among a handful of legislators who have spoken out against Kern's remarks. Lindley said he is not surprised, as he thinks there is significant homophobia in the Legislature, and those who are not themselves homophobic are intimidated by a vocal faction who are.

Chris Benge said Kern, "has a right to express her opinion."

Asked whether her comments represent the House Republican caucus, Benge said, "Each member has their own opinion, there's no way that I can say whether that reflects the rest of the Republican caucus or not."

It's at this point a round of thoughts fire back and forth in my mind. Well, to give him the benefit of the diplomatic doubt because he seems to be such a great all around kind of guy, maybe by chance Rep. Benge hasn't read the Republican Party "Grassroots" Platform? Sad for me to say but I can show him exactly where to look in the Oklahoma Republican Party Platform to find a lot of official grassroots homophobia, it's spelled out in very large unmistakable – those "aberrant" gays will never be tolerated in Oklahoma - print!

It's painful to think this, but I guess it shouldn't surprise me that possibly some republicans may not be reading what's in their own party platform because it's now starting to become regrettably clear that, by their actions, many of those staunch conservative Christian Republicans don't seem to be reading or comprehending the teachings of Jesus Christ very much either. And while shaking my courage to its core, I'm forced to wonder if some of these people are the False Christians the Bible warns me of? I'm staring this question in the Oklahoma Bulls-eye because my Bible tells me very straight-forwardly in 1 John 3:10 "This is how we know who the children of God are and who the children of the devil are. Anyone who does not do right (by understanding and forgiving his brother) is not a child of God; nor is anyone who does not love his brother." And to really "do the right thing" there's Luke 6:31/35-36

"Do unto others as you would have them do unto you...But love your enemies, do good to them...Be merciful, just as your Father is merciful."

And here's a major conflict, if the Republican Party in Oklahoma has declared a Holy War against Homosexuals and homosexuals are to be considered "the enemy" then if these conservative republicans are True Christians shouldn't they be doing good things with good will toward all homosexuals? Shouldn't their party platform show mercy toward homosexuals? Shouldn't they, if they were True, be doing unto homosexuals as they would have others - now do unto them? The Holy Spirit within me tells me, "Yes, yes, and very plainly YES!"

And in Romans 12:13-16 "Share with God's people who are in need. Practice hospitality. Bless those who persecute you; bless and do not curse. Rejoice with those who rejoice; mourn with those who mourn. Live in harmony with one another. Do not be proud but be willing to associate with people of low position. Do not be conceited."

And here's another very serious blow in this fight for what is right – if the Bible says, "do not be proud but be willing to associate with people of low position... do not be conceited" then did the Oklahoma Legislators who refused to accept as a love offering an honorary copy of the Qur'an from the Muslim community here in Oklahoma; well, did these proud Christian legislators commit serious hypocrisy by not being willing to associate with people they judge (?) to be of low position? Yes, because Sally Kern stated, "homosexuality is worse than terrorism or Islam" Are Muslims and homosexuals, to one degree or another, now both to be considered the enemies? Yet, that's twice the number of enemies – so doesn't it mean - in no uncertain terms - that conservative Christian republicans should be showing and expressing twice the love while having twice the enemies? Yes, so help me God, it does! But no.... I am still seeing hate and division here in Oklahoma instead of feeling simple love and pure grace. So now I'm bound to fire back and ask, was it those people's own personal conceit that made them refuse in front of the whole world to associate themselves with the Muslim faith, Muslim people, or for that matter anyone else they are now proud to judge and call – "the enemy?" And again the Holy Spirit shouts in my mind... James 4:11-12 "Brothers , do NOT slander one another. Anyone who speaks against his brother or judges him speaks against the law and judges it. When you judge the law you are NOT keeping it, but sitting IN judgment on it. There is only one Lawgiver and Judge, the one who is able to save and destroy – BUT YOU – WHO ARE YOU TO JUDGE YOUR NEIGHBOR?"

Then as I remember the frightful words of Diane Habersaat, in her defense of Sally Kern, "The people are being intimidated and terrorized by all the "Gay Rights" groups who are pushing to get hate crimes legislation passed whereby our freedom of speech will be silenced along with our ability to preach the truth from God's word." So I personally think of the biblical truth about that, yes, there are parts of the Bible that condemn homosexuality but there are also parts of the Bible that stress as in 1 Corinthians 13:4-7 "Love is patient, love is kind. It does not envy, it does not boast, it is not proud. It is not rude, it is not self-seeking, it is not easily angered, it keeps NO record of wrong. Love does not delight in evil but rejoices with the truth. It always protects, always trusts, always hopes, always perseveres." And I wonder about how so many Christians seem to pick and choose only those parts of the Bible that they want to emphasize in their effort to be able to demonize homosexuals or Muslims while totally ignoring the fact that the Bible also teaches that love always protects.... So why won't they, if they're Truly Good Christians, protect and embrace another prime concept found in the Holy Bible....

Acts 15:8-11 "God who knows the heart showed that he accepted them by giving the Holy Spirit to them just as he did to us. He made no distinction between us and them, for – He purified their hearts by faith. Now then, why do you try to test God by putting on the necks of disciples a yoke that neither we nor our fathers have been able to bear? No – WE BELIEVE IT IS THROUGH THE GRACE OF OUR LORD JESUS THAT WE ARE SAVED – JUST AS THEY ARE!" And in Romans 13:10 "Love does no harm to its neighbor, therefore love IS the fulfillment of the law." And as I think about how harmful the Republican Party Platform is to homosexuals.... I meditate on John 7:24 "STOP JUDGING BY MERE APPERANCES AND MAKE A RIGHT JUDGMENT." So I fight with myself over why so many judgmental Christians talk so much about being able to, "preach the truth from God's word" yet they themselves don't even listen to "the truth from God's word"?

And my mind goes certifiably crazy... especially when I KNOW love is also supposed to trust... so above it all I wonder – why won't judgmental Christians TRUST the American Psychological Association when the mental health experts tell us that, as in the words of my own personal therapist, "There is NOTHING WRONG with being a homosexual – There is NOTHING ABNORMAL about being homosexual – There is NO REASON to feel ashamed for being a homosexual!"

But, it's here I finally again remember: I'm not supposed to judge judgmental Christians anymore than they are supposed to be judging ANYONE else! And it's with all of these internal battles raging that I find myself starting to be disabled by the stark terrors of it all. Yet, I still have to confess contrary to some people's opinions I personally think the worst kind of terror is not really homosexuality or Islam. I imagine the very worst kind of terror is to experience the terror of when we honestly look at our own selves in the mirror and finally become fully-conscious to the fact that our own personal judgments were way out of line while we're totally sleeping to the self-conceit that Satan is spawning within us. One day, hopefully, we will all awaken to the truth and realize these Holy Wars are able to continue on and on.... only because we've allowed ourselves to be blindingly biased by Satan. And yes, I ask, is Satan still seducing us by way of his using our very own self-glorifying thoughts of mind – against us one and all?

But, even now as all of these very different and frightful notions collide in my consciousness I can still thank God, for He has graciously sent to me a doctor, a very important doctor - someone I believe was destined to come just to save my very fractured and freaked-out independent state of mind! And I do have to admit my mind right now IS very fractured and divided over the different kinds of Oklahomans I've now met and those I've heard of. And what a spiritual lesson, for me, to be right here - right now - just to see the contrasts in Christians and how, thank God, 70 percent of the average-Joe-Okies are for the common gay man to still get a fair shake in the Great State of Oklahoma....you know, that state where the grace-filled wind comes whipping down the plains... we only hope and pray that one day that loving grace-filled wind blows strong enough so that it can break through the Oklahoma capital doors with it's heavily reinforced mental barriers... and gently, lovingly the Holy Spirit's wind lands like tongues of Holy Enlightenment, giving and voluntarily sharing, while emotionally sinking deep into the brains of some of our Still Beloved but sometimes very Un-Christ-like Christian Legislators' heads.

Yes, dear Lord, like you did for Saul, please remove the scales that are blinding anyone's eyes to the fact that Satan, "Masquerading as apostles of Christ", is alive and well while circling our many American Capital domes and Satan is the one who has really convinced some of our people of their own "superior Christian position" – and, dear God, how sad for anyone's soul that un-like Christ – someone could want to take that superior position of power and trust and establish a worldly government that considers it legally binding and right to cast stones at any people who are at any point politically vulnerable and more defenseless than they! The Holy Spirit reminds me, "It's NOT – CHRISTIAN for the Republican Goliath to ever pounce on such easy political-prey targets!

And then, in a quick turn of thoughts, I now have to do a little spiritual rejoicing because of all of the very many good hearted and Christ-like Oklahomans I've personally met; yes, I know why Oklahoma is still called the "heartland," even in spite of the fact that some of our Legislators appear to have NO heart! So maybe with the double edge perception of war, maybe I need to re-adjust my view to realize that war CAN bring out the best in people… it brings out the best of compassion for those little children considered to be just, "collateral damage"… it brings out the best sense of unity to fight a common enemy! I just pray that for all the people in the world who now claim to be devotedly Christian and who claim to read and want to "spread the word" while teaching the Holy Bible… would these fine people be willing to totally embrace just one of the most powerful quotes found in the field called the Holy Bible, Luke 3:6

"And ALL MANKIND will see God's salvation!"

Yes, dear Lord, thank you that since it IS written in the Holy Bible that all mankind will be saved… so armed with the biblical knowledge that ALL WILL BE SAVED, that verse plainly tells me my brother is NOT my enemy – my enemy number one is now ONLY Satan – the Proud!

And thank You, Honorable Lord, for all of Your Children who fully understand the true power of - the Salvation of ALL – all done by Your Grace and Mercy – so that NO ONE MAY BOAST! And dear God, no matter how many times I am cursed to hell by my fellow brothers or sisters I thank you my Father that Your Love will still eventually win out for us all. And thank you, dear God, for giving me the exposure to so many honest examples of Your Mercy with ALL OF THE MANY QUOTES sometimes hidden deep within Your Bible, that for those who seek, they will find, time after time… quote after quote…. once the False is separated from the True in the Bible.... The only message that is repeated the most are all the "quotes" calling for us to have ETERNAL HOPE!

And I DO have hope in John 12:32 (Jesus said) "But I, when I am lifted up from the earth, will draw ALL MEN to myself."

So, as I think of "Eternal Hope" the Holy Spirit tells me to read in the Jesus Christ containing - Holy Qur'an verse 5:48 "If God had so willed, He would have created you one community, but [He has not done so] that He may test you in what He has given you, so compete with one another in good works. To God you shall ALL return and He will tell you the truth about that which you have been disputing."

Then once again, in my Holy Spirit's off-balancing sense of humor, my Spirit tells me that God DOES forgive even homosexuals because it is His Ultimate True Test to ALL RELIGIONS... to see if we can ALL finally see beyond our own noses to truly practice what we preach.... when the bottom-line of conservative salvation is ALL about the full understanding of what to "FORGIVE YOUR BROTHER" really means!

And thank you God, that with me also understanding A Course in Miracles, If Grace is True, and now when I re-focus my teachings of the Holy Bible I see that EVERYONE has the seed of love buried so deep inside of us that we'll never ever be able to truly run away from Your Love for too long!

But regretfully on also reflecting that, too many times, I've had to.... RUN FOR MY LIFE FROM SOME OF YOUR CHRISTIANS, it seems that my personal private mental battle is "In the World of Politics" still doomed to continue......

Dr. Westen's Shot Heard All Around the World...

During the course of any war many different kinds of shots are fired. Some shots are fired used only in self-defense while other more sinister shots are aimed strictly to cripple by premeditated attack. Some shots are the inner kinds of shots that can wound your soul or can emotionally kill you to you hear.... Thankfully, more merciful shots are the kinds of shots that potentially will save us all from Satan's selfish-thought producing False Christian illusions.

So, while throwing heavier competitive ideologies back and forth in my mind, I suddenly realize just how wounded I've become with all of this constant in-fighting, so I prayed to my heavenly Commander in Chief and I decided I quickly needed to find me a life saving medic.

And by the grace of God, I found a doctor who instead of prescribing another pill he just gave me something very important to mentally chew on. But upon seeing the wreck of a holy-terror I was in, this compassionate but battle-experienced doctor decided I also needed an extremely realistic dose of even heavier cerebral contemplation. This respected and highly decorated veteran of many harsh holy-wars is named Dr. Drew Westen.

But, for me, upon seeing the very powerful syringe he held in his hands, I reconsidered while asking with a half-brave face, "Are you sure you want to stick that potent of a dose directly into me?" But without blinking, he looked me straight in the eyes as he replied, "Do you want to get better or not? If you do - drop your damn defenses!" He then warned me, "Now steady your nerves and get ready" while he took a deep jab at everyone's common human weaknesses! And yes inwardly I cried, "Oh my dear God," because Dr. Westen gave me such a powerful shot of cerebral contemplation that I can still feel it penetrating even to this day!

But, after receiving my mental-life saving dose while I was in the process of pulling up my pants unexpectedly my jaw just totally dropped! And I wondered with my jaw dropping like it did was it a by-product of knowing after all this is said and done, someone's going to have a very chapped and sore ass? Or, was my jaw dropping just a completely natural reaction related to the fact that I've finally been told the gospel of political-mental health rules – And yes, I DO BELIEVE, so…. this is so very important – this doctor's report could turn out to be our sanity-saving honest to God medical proof that there's drastic blindness caused by self inner-bias!

MSNBC.com "Political bias affects brain activity, study finds."

Democrats and Republican both adept at ignoring facts, brain scans show – Jan. 24th 2006

"Democrats and Republicans alike are adept at making decisions without letting the facts get in the way, a new study shows. And they get quite a rush from ignoring information that's contrary to their point of view.

Researchers asked staunch party members from both sides to evaluate information that threatened their preferred candidate prior to the 2004 Presidential election. The subjects' brains were monitored while they pondered. The results were announced today. "We did not see any increased activation of the parts of the brain normally engaged during reasoning," said Drew Westen, director of clinical psychology at Emory University. "What we saw instead was a network of emotion circuits lighting up, including circuits hypothesized to be involved in regulating emotion, and circuits known to be involved in resolving conflicts." – BIAS ON BOTH SIDES –

The test subjects on both sides of the political aisle reached totally biased conclusions by ignoring information that could not rationally be discounted, Westen and his colleagues say. Then, with their minds made up, brain activity ceased in the areas that deal with negative emotions such as disgust. But activity spiked in the circuits involved in reward, a response similar to what addicts experience when they get a fix, Westen explained. The study points to a total lack of reason in political decision-making.

"None of the circuits involved in conscious reasoning were particularly engaged," Westen said. "Essentially, it appears as if partisans twirl the cognitive kaleidoscope until they get the conclusions they want, and then they get massively reinforced for it, with the elimination of negative emotional states and activation of positive ones." Notably absent were any increases in activation of the dorsolateral prefrontal cortex, the part of the brain most associated with reasoning. The tests involved pairs of statements by the candidates, President George W. Bush and Senator John Kerry, that clearly contradict each other. The test subjects were asked to consider and rate the discrepancy. Then they were presented with another statement that might explain away the contradiction. The scenario was repeated several times for each candidate. A brain-scan technique known as functional magnetic resonance imaging, or FMRI, revealed a consistent pattern. Both Republicans and Democrats consistently denied obvious contradictions for their own candidate but detected contradictions in the opposing candidate. "The result is that partisan beliefs are calcified, and the person can learn very little from new data," Westen said.

Other relatively neutral candidates were introduced into the mix, such as the actor Tom Hanks. Importantly, both the Democrats and Republicans reacted to the contradictions of these characters in the same manner. The findings could prove useful beyond the campaign trail.

"Everyone from executives and judges to scientists and politicians may reason to emotionally biased judgments when they have a vested interest in how to interpret 'the facts,'" Westen said.

And as I personally contemplate on Dr. Westen's medical facts and the fact that in our troubled Holy War kind of world it seems way too many times - "the facts will always be fixed around any human's inner self-gratifying policy."

So decisions, decisions, what should I now think? What does my bias believe? I believe, like Dr. Drew Westen pointed out to me, "The result is that partisan beliefs are calcified, and the person can learn very little from new data!" And then like a P.O.W., it hits me, how ironic that science is now re-interpreting the Bible while some biased Christian politicians are promoting un-Christ-like justice and giving Christianity - such a bad name! Also to my continuing horror, so many of the Christian Churches are now bowing down to a sad gospel of grace-destroying UN-educated hate!

And as I contemplate on calcified partisan beliefs and people who choose to learn very little of the new... I think of the Bible's parable of putting new wine into an old wine skin and I am again reminded of the blind who are willfully, comfortably biased but unnervingly I think of how my head is now starting to get a little woozy and I'm very lite-headed. And as I try to maintain clarity, with my brain seeming to be reeling, I realize Dr. Drew Westen's strong shot of contemplation may now have just kicked-started my very fertile imaginative thought-processes and I'm afraid it'll have very serious and far reaching global consequences.

So in deciding I quickly needed to just lay-down and rest, soon I find myself fighting to stumble out the front door as I leave Dr. Drew's infirmary to make my way home to the barracks hoping to recover from all of this war related arguing with a little bit of shut eye. But as I finally make my way to safety and what I hope will be a good night's sleep, yet the words of Dr. Drew Westen forevermore seem to be firing-off rapid succession in my mind. These words seem to have a very bombastic somber life... all of their own,

"All religions alike are adept at making judgments without letting the facts get in the way!"

"The test subjects on all sides of the religious spectrum reached totally biased conclusions by ignoring information that could not be rationally discounted."

"The study points to a total lack of reason in religious decision-making, "None of the circuits involved in conscious reasoning were particularly engaged, essentially. It appears as if religious zealots twirl the cognitive kaleidoscope until they get massively reinforced for it, with the elimination of negative emotional states and activation of positive ones" – kind of like a drug addict getting a "superior-high."

"The tests involved statements from different Holy Books that clearly contradicted each other.... It seems all religious zealots consistently denied obvious contradictions for their own Holy Book but detected contradictions in other people's saviors!"

"The result is that religious beliefs are calcified, unbending, and the person can learn very little from new data. The findings could prove useful to understand why people try so hard to convince and convert others to their own personal beliefs. Everyone from Christians to Muslims to Jews and their politicians may reason to emotionally biased judgments when they have a vested interest in how to interpret the facts over the basic concept of salvation!"

But suddenly in a quiet moment of spiritual calm I realize - right now I can no longer fight over the concept of who we need to be "SAVED FROM": if it's gays and lesbians or those damning False Christians or just Democrats or Republicans - Arab or Jew! So dear God, I lift up both my hands high in the air and, giving up, honestly right now, still spinning from Dr. Drew's shot, the only fact I can focus on is... the fact that, after all I've just been through, I now know I've totally lost my mind!

So still grappling with myself, with what seems like tons of protective arms all around me, assisting me, I slowly try to lay me down to sleep to dream the night away, on my dear old worn out military issued cot I find myself tossing and turning what seems is the whole night through. First to the left and then violently to the right I hear so many convincing, demanding sets of screams and Christian battle plans.... And, while contemplating if those screams are really "theirs" or "mine".... by bombs' bitter blasts and foggy flair's light in this dream lacking any real sanity I so do wonder – with all of this god-awful political and religiously master-minded hell of a conflict continuing to wage on.... where in this nightmare is my truly good first rate General Christian? Any good humble General Christian who will help to put an end to this horribly cursed war will do – yes, someone self-sacrificing like Jesus the Christ! Someone who is wise enough and Truly Compassionate enough to graciously say, "I am so secure in my own religious beliefs that anytime you're around me, even if you worship different - in any way, I still like you and will honor you and I PROMISE not to pass punishing laws against you .... And instead, you always have the legal freedom to verbally express, to the wholeness of society, your own God-given al be it sometimes nutty views!"

But as I remember that the devil's always in the details.... I can't help but to muffle a scream loudly to myself... as I purposely close my eyes to invite deep sleep, I pray thee Lord my soul to keep, while thinking of the immense challenges of detailing everyone else's personal view of God... and of heaven.... and of hell... and for all of us in society.... What constitutes crossing the borderline to reach VERY insane-religious behavior? And as my own mind goes round and round I realize, damn it, now I know WHY I can't sleep.... I have yet to do the most important duty of my day. So I flip on the light by my military nightstand and tucked carefully close by me is my "A Course in Miracles" and opening up the mystical spiritual Satan-destroying war-fair book I spy, "Lesson for the day #185" ..... I want the peace of God.

And realizing how confused my mind is these days it's no wonder I can't sleep so I could sure use some of God's inner peace right now! So even in my partially sleep deprived and anti-depressant haze I intently focus and read from my battle field copy of A Course in Miracles in preparation for my next recon mission...

"I want the peace of God. To say these words is nothing. But to mean these words is everything. If you could but mean them for just an instant, there would be no further sorrow possible for you in any form, in any place or time. Heaven would be completely given back to full awareness, memory of God entirely restored, the resurrection of all creation fully recognized.

No one can mean these words and not be healed. He cannot play with dreams nor think he is himself a dream. He cannot make a hell and think it real. He wants the peace of God, and it is given him. For that is all he wants, and that is all he will receive. Many have said these words. But few indeed have meant them. You have but to look upon the world you see around you to be sure how very few they are. The world would be completely changed should any two agree these words express the only thing they want.

Two minds with one intent become so strong that what they will becomes the Will of God. For minds can only join in truth. In dreams no two can share the same intent. To each the hero of the dream is different; the outcome wanted not the same for both. Loser and gainer merely shift about in changing patterns, as the ratio of gain to loss and loss to gain takes on a different aspect of another form.

Yet compromise alone a dream can bring. Sometimes it takes the form of union, but only the form. The meaning must escape the dream, for compromising is the goal of dreaming. Minds cannot unite in dreams. They merely bargain. And what bargain can give them the peace of God? Illusions come to take His place. And what He means is lost to sleeping minds intent on compromise, each to his gain and to another's loss.

To mean you want the peace of God is to renounce all dreams. For no one means these words who wants illusions and who therefore seeks the means which bring illusions. He has looked on them and found them wanting. Now he seeks to go beyond them, recognizing that another dream would offer nothing more than all the others. Dreams are one to him. And he has learned their only difference is one of form, for one will bring the same despair and misery as do the rest.

The mind which means that all it wants is peace must join with other minds, for that is how peace is obtained. And when the wish for peace is genuine, the means for finding it are given in a form each mind which seeks for it in honesty can understand. Whatever form the lesson takes is planned for him in such a way that he can not mistake it if his asking is sincere. And if he asks without sincerity, there is no form in which the lesson will meet with acceptance and be truly learned.

Let us today devote our practicing to recognizing that we really mean the words we say. We want the peace of God. This is no idle wish. These words do not request another dream be given us. They do not ask for compromise nor try to make another bargain in the hope that there may yet be one which can succeed where all the rest have failed. To mean these words acknowledges illusions are in vain, requesting the eternal in place of shifting dreams which seem to change in what they offer, but are one in nothingness.

Today devote your practice periods to careful searching of your mind to find the dreams you cherish still. What do you ask for in your heart? Forget the words you use in making your requests. Consider but what you believe will comfort you and bring you happiness. But be you not dismayed by lingering illusions, for their form is not what matters now. Let not some dreams be more acceptable, reserving shame and secrecy for others. They are one.

And being one, one question should be asked of all of them: "Is this what I would have, in place of Heaven and the peace of God?" This is the choice you make. Be not deceived that it is otherwise. No compromise is possible in this. You choose God's peace, or you have asked for dreams. And dreams will come as you requested them. Yet will God's peace come just as certainly and to remain with you forever. It will not be gone with every twist and turning of the road to reappear unrecognized in forms which shift and change with every step you take.

You want the peace of God. And so do all who seem to seek for dreams. For them as well as for yourself you ask but this when you make this request with deep sincerity. For thus you reach to what they really want and join your own intent with what they seek above all things, perhaps unknown to them, but sure to you. You have been weak at times, uncertain in your purpose and unsure of what you wanted, where to look for it, and where to turn for help in the attempt. Help has been given you. And would you not avail yourself of it by sharing it?

No one who truly seeks the peace of God can fail to find it. For he merely asks that he deceive himself no longer by denying to himself what is God's Will. Who can remain unsatisfied who asks for what he has already? Who could be unanswered who requests an answer which is his to give? The peace of God is yours.

For you it was created, given you by its Creator and established as His own eternal gift. How can you fail when you but ask for what He wills for you? And how could your request be limited to you alone? No gift of God can be unshared. It is this attribute that sets the gifts of God apart from every dream that ever seemed to take the place of truth.

No one can lose and everyone must gain whenever any gift of God has been requested and received by anyone. God gives but to unite. To take away is meaningless to Him. And when it is as meaningless to you, you can be sure you share One Will with Him, and He with you. And you will also know you share One Will with all your brothers, whose intent is yours.

It is this one intent we seek today, uniting our desires with the need of every heart, the call of every mind, the hope that lies beyond despair, the love attack would hide, the brotherhood that hate has sought to sever, but which still remains as God created it. With help like this beside us, can we fail today as we request the peace of God be given us?"

Then, as I finally lay my course of miracles down for the night, turning off the illuminating lamp; once again I curl up under my covers and repeat in my mind just to myself, "I want the peace of God, I want the peace of God to extend to all my brothers and sisters, I want the peace of God to surround the whole world with the blessings of emotional receptivity...." And even thou I try my damndest at finding that God given peace that passeth understanding, the demons from the dark side seem to be still taunting me from the comfort of my own barrack's bed. While they scream, "You're gonna get seriously CRUCIFIED for what you've now said and done – don't say we didn't WARN YOU..." so, without ANY of God's mercy, they continue to rip my self-worth apart with their words all the while making mean-spirited sadistic fun of me! And yet, while I'm now trying my holy-best to forget about all of the worldly fighting going on deep inside of my head, I cringe in my cot as I realize, tomorrow IS the start of a new and very important combat mission to restore TRUE-LOVE to the message of the TRUE-CHRIST who has the infinite capacity to love both TRUE and ALL FALSE CHRISTIANS completely... equally....

Yet, dear God, in the meantime, if I make it through this dark night of torture till redemption to live to yet fight another round of hotly contested-inner-battles please help me, my Father, to always treat any of those holy warriors who I might yet cross-paths with... with only Your God-given Christ-resurrected kind of Agape Love!"

So, for now, to all the world a peace filled good-night, then quietly, as I wonder laying in the protection of my freshly cleaned white cotton and metal bed, heck, what's that drip, drip, drip.... but right before I lose full consciousness, I at last feel the gentle caresses of the Holy Spirit flowing through me, warming and infusing me, while He whispers in total care-giver compassion, " We know how hard you've been bullied and shoved almost to the breaking point beyond soul repair - battling with all of Satan's many hates and his hell-of-a "psych-ops" war - but; TRUST US, you're in Seriously Healing Hands as of now ... so sleep-well... Good Christian Hunter!"

As my Spirit and I both say in unison, "Amen."

It's then – I finally, totally... surrender to the TRUE LOVE I can now sense!

And for the first time in a very, very long time... "I'm not AFRAID to fall asleep.....during this... dark and thunderous storm..... who's PROJECTING..... their own lack of love onto........

(to be continued)